Health Care
Reboot

Health Care
Reboot

Megatrends Energizing American Medicine

Michael J. Dowling
and Charles Kenney

ForbesBooks

Published by ForbesBooks, Charleston, South Carolina.
Member of Advantage Media Group.

ForbesBooks is a registered trademark, and the ForbesBooks colophon is a trademark of Forbes Media, LLC.

Printed in the United States of America.

10 9 8 7 6 5 4 3 2 1

ISBN: 978-1-946633-49-1
LCCN: 2018955821

This publication is designed to provide accurate and authoritative information in regard to the subject matter covered. It is sold with the understanding that the publisher is not engaged in rendering legal, accounting, or other professional services. If legal advice or other expert assistance is required, the services of a competent professional person should be sought.

Advantage Media Group is proud to be a part of the Tree Neutral® program. Tree Neutral offsets the number of trees consumed in the production and printing of this book by taking proactive steps such as planting trees in direct proportion to the number of trees used to print books. To learn more about Tree Neutral, please visit www.treeneutral.com.

Since 1917, the Forbes mission has remained constant. Global Champions of Entrepreneurial Capitalism. ForbesBooks exists to further that aim by bringing the Stories, Passion, and Knowledge of top thought leaders to the forefront. ForbesBooks brings you The Best in Business. To be considered for publication, please visit www.forbesbooks.com.

TABLE OF CONTENTS

CHAPTER ONE

Reboot: American Health Care Ascendant

"The Genie is out of the bottle."

For generations, certain foundational beliefs about America have girded the nation's confidence. Among these have been America as the land of opportunity, the rightness of our cause in the Cold War, and the conceit that the finest health care anywhere was to be found in the United States. For many years, civic and political leaders, seeing medical care under the banner of American exceptionalism, have declared US health care *the best in the world*.

In recent decades, however, this perception has been turned on its head. An ever-lengthening series of studies, books, and articles suggest that not only is the US not the best in the world, but that it is bloated, wasteful, and among the worst when compared with other industrialized nations. Lately this "American-health care-in-decline" narrative has taken root, and as it has done so the bill of indictment has grown longer and ever more scolding. Emblematic of the decline narrative is a book by Elisabeth Rosenthal, a physician and former *New York Times* reporter who serves as editor-in-chief of Kaiser Health

News. In the opening sentence of her book, *An American Sickness: How Healthcare Became Big Business and How You Can Take It Back*, she writes that America's "medical system has stopped focusing on health or even science. Instead, it attends more or less single-mindedly to its own profits."[1]

Rosenthal is unsparing in her critique of the system as "fantastically expensive, inefficient, bewildering, and inequitable," and "deeply, perhaps fatally, flawed." During the past twenty-five years, Rosenthal contends, health care in the US has gone from "a caring endeavor" to a point where "money became the metric of good medicine." In this "slow-moving heist," treatment "follows not scientific guidelines, but the logic of commerce," where "financial crimes [are] imposed on our bodies in the name of health."[2]

"Faced with disease," she writes, "we are all potential victims of medical extortion." President Trump appears to agree with at least some of Rosenthal's analysis, having declared that among other nations "everybody" has "better health care than we do."[3]

Rosenthal is hardly alone. One of the most successful businesspeople in the country, Charlie Munger, Warren Buffet's associate at Berkshire Hathaway, made the unfortunate accusation that many doctors "are artificially prolonging death so they can make more money." Health care analyst Paul Keckley writes of the "persistent media attention" to the "shortcomings and errors" of US health care, while *USA Today* flatly condemns the system as "nonsensical." While there is solid reporting in American media about health care, there is also an aspect to much coverage that is suffused with "suffocating negativism," as one prominent physician characterized it, that serves

---

1 Rosenthal, *An American Sickness: How Healthcare Became Big Business and How You Can Take It Back.*

2 Ibid.

3 Ibid.

largely to feed the decline narrative.[4]

Some of the most widely cited data supporting the decline narrative come from the Commonwealth Fund, which has published numerous studies marking the comparative inadequacy of the US system. In one report the Commonwealth Fund found that "despite having the most expensive health care system, the United States ranks last overall among eleven industrialized countries on measures of health system quality, efficiency, access to care, equity, and healthy lives."[5]

Reports from various sources sustain the narrative that the US ranks "70th among 132 nations in health and wellness"; that the country is "near last among 17 high-income nations in several categories," etc.[6]

On the surface, this grim portrait seems fair enough. In the US, we spend more per person than any country in the world, and there is evidence that too much of that money is wasted on overuse and administrative inefficiencies. Certainly, it is true that the existing care-delivery system is fragmented, sometimes dysfunctional, and nearly always complex. ("Unbelievably complex" in the words of the president, who made the somewhat surprising assertion that "nobody knew health care could be so complicated.")[7]

---

4   Keckley, "Myth No. 1: Quality of Care in the US Health System is the Best in the World."

5   The Commonwealth Fund, "US Health System Ranks Last Among Eleven Countries on Measures of Access, Equity, Quality, Efficiency, and Healthy Lives"; The other nations studied included Australia, Canada, France, Germany, the Netherlands, New Zealand, Norway, Sweden, Switzerland, and the United Kingdom. The survey found the US ranking "in the middle on quality of care."

6   Hagop Kantarjian, "An Unhealthy System."

7   Liptak, "Trump: 'Nobody knew health care could be so complicated.'"

While we take Elisabeth Rosenthal and other proponents of the decline narrative seriously, we have a different perspective; we argue in this book that the decline narrative is both outdated and overstated. We *do not* suggest that the system is without its shortcomings, but we contend that there is another side to the story—a side that is perhaps more nuanced, and surely more upbeat, than the decline narrative. We argue in this book that American health care is actually on a positive pathway, but that the decline narrative's shroud of negativity makes it more difficult to discern innovations and improvements. By no means are we myopic about the system's flaws. We see the imperfections daily in our own organization. At the same time, we see compelling evidence of progress in a series of major trends that, taken together, have the US on a positive new course. Each of the trends we write about provides an important support beam in a rapidly changing infrastructure undergirding the overall health care system. While we believe in the individual strength of these trends, it is their collective power that has us convinced that something new and exciting is happening; that our nation is constructing a solid foundation upon which the new American health care is being erected. Yes, our health care system has many problems, but there has been significant progress, and new developments hold the promise of better, more affordable care.

We confess to being optimistic about the direction in which health care is headed, and we're aware that this sort of optimism has "gone out of style," as writer Gregg Easterbrook puts it. (Easterbrook's view is that optimism should "become intellectually respectable again.")[8]

Steven Pinker, the Harvard cognitive psychologist, helps widen

---

8   Gregg Easterbrook, *It's Better Than it looks: Reasons for Optimism in an Age of Fear.*

the lens through which we see health care today. Pinker is an outlier—an avowed optimist in this time of negativity. In his book *Enlightenment Now: The Case for Reason, Science, Humanism, and Progress,* Pinker writes that "optimism is not generally thought cool, and it is often thought foolish." Yet Pinker expresses boundless optimism for the direction of the world as he celebrates historical advances of recent centuries.[9]

On a more modest scale, we make a similar case with respect to the direction of health care in the United States. Pinker sees the world through a different lens for a fresher perspective that counters in some ways the toxicity that marks the current discourse in many fields and, too often, in health care, as well. Pinker writes of progress "that is easy to miss while we are living through it," and we believe that applies directly to the progress in health care over recent decades. He observes that "the second half of the second decade of the third millennium would not seem to be an auspicious time to publish a book on the historical sweep of progress and its causes. At the time of this writing, my country is led by people with a dark vision of the current moment." But Pinker seeks to "show that this bleak assessment of the state of the world is wrong. And not just a little wrong—wrong, wrong, flat-earth wrong, couldn't-be-more-wrong." We found Pinker's book a *tour de force* that delivers on that promise.[10]

Our book takes a narrower slice of more recent history, but we see thematic similarities, and we also see this as an ideal time to write about the positive trends in health care. Many of these trends, as we shall see in the chapters to come, are aligning to put the US on a pathway to better, safer, more accessible care. We make our

---

9   Steven Pinkner, *Enlightenment Now: The Case for Reason, Science, Humanism, and Progress.*

10   Ibid.

case in the hopes that readers of all stripes—health care professionals delivering care, patients receiving care, businesspeople purchasing care, as well as government officials who both purchase care and set health care policy—will recognize the newly encouraging direction of the industry and work to accelerate the evolution of these trends. We have aspired to write the book in as clear-eyed and non-technical a manner as possible in the hopes of persuading the widest-possible audience to our point of view. We believe that while the trends we write about are quite powerful, they are not necessarily self-sustaining. These trends require more than a degree of nurturing as well as the support of health care stakeholders who are either receiving, delivering, or paying for care. For our belief is that if the trends can be accelerated and sustained over time, we will move more quickly to a new and much better delivery system. If the trends stall, important progress will have been lost.

Our optimism is based on the progress we have seen in recent decades. We want to make crystal clear our belief that the US health care system is far from perfect, that there are major quality, safety, access, and equity challenges. But the decline narrative fails to recognize the other reality—that the quality movement in health care has succeeded in making great strides in all of those areas; that the men and women at the frontlines of care who are innovating and finding new ways of delivering better care should be acknowledged and, more than that, celebrated!

Consider just a few indicators of progress during the past twenty or so years. From 2000 to 2012, the US achieved more than a 30 percent decline in the death rates for heart disease and stroke. While cancer deaths climbed throughout most of the twentieth century, the trend has been reversed. Since the 1990s cancer deaths have declined by an estimated 16 percent. And care is safer.[11]

"From 2010 to 2015, incidents of patient harm such as infections, falls, and traumas in hospitals fell by 21 percent nationally resulting in an estimated 3.1 million fewer hospital-acquired conditions and infections, 125,000 fewer patients dying in hospitals, and nearly $28 billion in cost savings."[12]

Dr. Robert Wachter, chair of the department of medicine at the University of California at San Francisco, and one of the leading experts on safety in the United States, told the *Boston Globe* that "there is no question that [health care] is safer for all sorts of reasons."[13]

Major advances have come in quality, safety, access, and performance measurement. And against the metrics supporting the decline narrative is the reality on the ground: millions of Americans get great care from dedicated doctors, nurses, and other caregivers every day.

Writing on *The Health Care Blog*, Paul Keckley cites a number of surveys in which the American people affirm their confidence in the quality of care they receive. Keckley also found a degree of optimism when he travelled to Dana Point, California, for a summit meeting of health care leaders ("arguably the most significant gathering of influentials across our industry") and found that "the tone was positive. All see a future state that's dramatically improved over the current state. They're optimistic but realistic: they recognize we're a long way from getting there. They envision a new system that balances care for the sick with health and wellbeing for the rest."[14]

We do not dispute the Commonwealth Fund and other leading

---

11 Sidney, et al., "Recent Trends in Cardiovascular Mortality in the United States and Public Health Goals."

12 Fryhofer et al., "Progress and Path Forward on Delivery System Reform."

13 Liz Kowalczyk, "Report Faults Children's Hospital for Medication Errors."

14 Keckley, "Radical Incrementalism or System Redesign: Which Way Foreward for US Healthcare."

organizations that suggest holes in the system, but at the same time it is clearly true that the United States has a far more diverse population—and far larger population—than any of the countries to which it is generally compared. Critics of our assertion that the US is ascending reasonably argue that the recent multiple-year decline in average US life expectancy—most recently from 78.7 years to 78.6 years in 2016—suggests a flawed medical system, and surely medicine broadly speaking deserves some blame.[15]

But it is also true that factors outside the direct control of doctors and hospitals play an outsized role. Joseph Newhouse, a Harvard health economist, told the *New York Times* that "medical care is one of the less important determinants of life expectancy. Socioeconomic status and other social factors exert larger influences on longevity."[16]

A 2018 report examined declining life-expectancy in the US and found its causes more complex than a failure of the country's health-delivery system. The report concludes:

> Many factors contribute to the health disadvantage; for example, Americans are more likely to engage in unhealthy behaviors (such as heavy caloric intake, drug abuse, and firearm ownership), live in cities designed for cars rather than pedestrians or cyclists, have weaker social-welfare supports, and lack universal health insurance.[17]

The report noted that Americans had a "high rate of death from both drug abuse (due to the opioid epidemic) and suicide" and that

---

15 Kochanek, et al., "Mortality in the United States, 2016."; The Centers for Disease Control and Prevention found that average life expectancy at birth fell in 2016 by 0.1 years, to 78.6, after a similar drop in 2015.

16 Frakt, "Medical Mystery: Something Happened to US Health Spending After 1980."

17 Cuckler et al., "National Health Expenditure Projections, 2017–26: Despite Uncertainty, Fundamentals Primarily Drive Spending Growth."

America's "social contract is weaker than in other countries—those in need have less access to social services, health care, or the prevention and treatment of mental illness and addiction.[18]

It is also worth noting that studies on mortality include both car accidents and gun violence, and Americans are much more likely to die of both causes than people in other countries. These are disturbing facts, but should car accidents and homicides play a role in characterizing a nation's health care quality? Gregory Mankiw, former chairman of the Council of Economic Advisors, has observed that differences in outcomes between the US and other nations—Canada, for example—"has more to do with broader social forces." Mankiw writes that the high rate of auto accidents and gun-related deaths "have lessons for traffic laws and gun control, but they teach us nothing about our system of health care ... The bottom line is that many statistics on health outcomes say little about our system of health care."[19]

An essential element of the decline narrative portrays the US system as the most expensive, and it is, indeed, a *very* expensive system. Americans spend double per person what other advanced nations spend. Various factors contribute to cost, including the aging of the population, technological innovations, consumer demand, and more. There is another side to the story which is generally unmentioned in the decline narrative.

David Cutler, the Harvard health economist, has plumbed the depths of whether "the benefits of medicine [are] worth what we pay for it." He writes that "even if there is waste and we could do better than we have, what we do is actually quite valuable. We have developed a modern 'medical industrial complex' that is incredibly

---

18   Ibid.
19   Mankiw, "Beyond those Healthcare Numbers."

> "Even if there is waste and we could do better than we have, what we do is actually quite valuable. We have developed a modern 'medical industrial complex' that is incredibly expensive, but also extremely productive."

expensive, but also extremely productive." Along with the waste, he says, "there is great value as well [and] … as a whole, the value far outweighs the waste."[20]

Gregory Mankiw echoes Cutler's view, writing that "increasing expenditures could just as well be a symptom of success. The reason that we spend more than our grandparents did is not waste, fraud, and abuse, but advances in medical technology and growth in incomes. Science has consistently found new ways to extend and improve our lives. Wonderful as they are, they do not come cheap."[21]

And while there is a common assumption that health care is riddled with waste—and there surely is waste in the system—it is also worth noting that the $3 trillion-plus dollars contributes mightily to the US economy in multiple positive ways, including providing well-paying jobs with good benefits for millions of Americans. (As the late Princeton economist Uwe Reinhardt put it: "In health care, one person's cost is another person's income.")[22]

In the fourth quarter of 2017, "for the first time in history, health care has surpassed manufacturing and retail, the most significant job engines of the 20th century, to become the largest source of jobs in the US."[23] The nation's recovery from the 2007–2008 economic crisis was aided by growth in health-sector jobs, which grew between 2006

20 Cutler, "Are the Benefits of Medicine Worth What We Pay for It?"
21 Mankiw, op. cit.
22 Reinhardt, "Health Reform in America."
23 Thompson, "Healthcare Just Became the US's Largest Employer."

and 2016 "at a rate of growth almost seven times faster than the rest of the economy … Health care jobs are still projected to grow at three times the rate of the rest of the economy during the next decade … Between 2016 and 2026, 15 of the 30 fastest-growing occupations nationally will be in health care, including four of the top six."[24]

There are examples of health systems and physician practices that have improved quality and reduced cost (including examples from within our own health system). And if the trends we write about continue and are accelerated, then better care at lower cost will be achievable on a broad scale in the years to come. Pursuing lower cost care—reducing unnecessary costs in the system—is essential to achieving high value care. This presents a challenge as the US population steadily ages and the demand for health services increases. The most recent projections from the federal government are a rude awakening: the Centers for Medicare & Medicaid Services reports that "national health spending is projected to grow 5.5 percent annually on average in 2017–26 and to represent 19.7 percent of the economy in 2026. Projected national health spending and enrollment growth over the next decade is largely driven by fundamental economic and demographic factors: changes in projected income growth, increases in prices for medical goods and services, and enrollment shifts from private health insurance to Medicare that are related to the aging of the population."[25]

In the near term, the best that can be hoped for is to manage the *rate* of spending increase. In the longer term, however, there is a growing consensus among health care professionals that it will be possible to improve value for the ten percent of the population that

---

24 US Bureau of Labor Statistics, "Fastest Growing Occupations."

25 Cuckler, et al., "National Health Expenditure Projections, 2017–26: Despite Uncertainty, Fundamentals Primarily Drive Spending Growth."

accounts for a majority of all costs and, in so doing, begin to bend the cost curve over time.

The most compelling evidence contradicting the decline narrative comes in the form of tangible improvements in quality and access. In recent years, improvements have come from fundamental changes in the way doctors and their teams care for patients. Traditional care was generally passive: a doctor waiting in a clinic or hospital for sick people to arrive and then treating them. The new American medicine is proactive and has physicians working in teams with nurses and other caregivers to reach out to patients and guide them along a pathway to health and wellbeing. At the same time, meaningful indicators of quality have improved. Hospital re-admission rates, for example, have declined. Behind these re-admission statistics is a movement throughout American health care in which physicians and their colleagues are embracing a broader role in patient care: improving the quality of care by better planning for patients before, during, and after visits and hospital stays.[26]

> **The new American medicine is proactive and has physicians working in teams with nurses and other caregivers to reach out to patients and guide them along a pathway to health and wellbeing.**

"This is a change in the mindset of doctors and hospitals that recognize they have responsibility for patients after they have been discharged," says Bill Kramer, executive director for national health policy at the Pacific Business Group on Health. "It is a recognition of a broader accountability for quality care." And while Kramer sees

---

26 Kamal, "Medicare Thirty-Day Hospital Readmission Rates Have Declined."

much room for improvement, he believes that there have been broad advances in quality and access, as well as progress among employers who collectively fund care for 178 million workers and their dependents. Large employers including Boeing, Walmart, Intel, and Lowe's, for example, have done a great job as innovators, he told us. These and other companies have identified new ways to partner with doctors and hospitals to improve care for their employees while also controlling costs.[27]

Among the most important improvements during the past two decades has been a focus on patients with multiple chronic conditions, such as congestive heart failure, diabetes, and cancer—the 10 percent of patients who account for a majority of all costs. Increasingly, medical groups throughout the nation work upstream to improve health and control costs. This more proactive approach is a step forward in improving care for these high-need, high-cost patients. In part, care is better due to greater focus by doctors on improved metrics used to measure quality, especially outcome measures that matter most to patients.

Technology has improved as well. While electronic medical records contribute to physician burnout, these systems also enable a new level of care coordination. And while the IT front in health care is often disruptive, there have been important advances that help improve quality and coordination. While care is not as safe as it needs to be or can be, it is nonetheless much safer than two decades ago when the Institute of Medicine of the National Academies issued its landmark report defining the frightening scope of medical errors in the US. Hospital-acquired infections, for example, had reached alarming proportions by the end of the 1990s, but a fulsome effort nationwide to adopt effective standard practices has reduced the risk

27   Bill Kramer, interview with author.

of such infections. The Centers for Disease Control and Prevention found that between 2008 and 2014, hospitals in the United States reduced health care-acquired infections (bacteria that infect patients while they are being treated). During that period, central-line associated bloodstream infections were reduced by 50 percent while surgical-site infections were cut by 17 percent, *C. difficile* infections were reduced by 8 percent (2011–2014), and deadly MRSA infections were reduced by 13 percent (2011–2014).[28]

While care has become safer, it has also become more accessible thanks in large measure to the Affordable Care Act, which made it possible for an additional twenty million Americans to gain coverage. In fact, the rate of uninsured Americans is at an historic low. As of early 2018, 91 percent of Americans had health insurance coverage. Coverage doesn't equal health in all cases, but this is nonetheless an important leap forward. (While many of those people are now covered by Medicaid, the reality is that the government pays only a portion—and in many cases a fraction—of the actual cost of delivering care to these patients. This places a heavy financial burden on hospitals and physician groups that provide the care.)[29]

The mindset of American health care stakeholders changed in 1999 when the Institute of Medicine issued its report, "To Err Is Human," indicating that as many as ninety-eight thousand preventable deaths occurred each year in the nation's hospitals. Reports on the study blanketed the nation's evening newscasts and daily newspapers and rocked the confidence of many physicians who believed that they and their institutions were providing excellent care. The result

---

28   Centers for Disease Control and Prevention, "HAI Data and Statistics."

29   Henry J. Kaiser Family Foundation, "Health Insurance Coverage of the Total Population."

of the report was an explosion in the modern movement to promote quality and safety, which was spawned in the late 1980s and early 1990s with the creation of the Pacific Business Group on Health, the Institute for Healthcare Improvement, and other groups.

The health care quality movement both acknowledged the scope of the problem with the safety and quality of care and vowed to make improvements throughout the land. In the nearly two decades since that report, hundreds of thousands of men and women throughout health care have invested countless hours working on innovations and improvements. Modest, individual changes and innovations in clinics and on inpatient floors have multiplied through the years thanks to frontline staff members finding new and better ways to care for patients. Over time, these discrete improvements, tens of thousands of them from coast-to-coast in large and small hospitals, in urban and rural physician practices, have improved quality and safety.

In 2018, analyst Paul Keckley observed:

> The quality improvement movement in the US system has had profound impact. Clinicians and academicians have improved clinical processes for diagnosing and treating specific patient populations, addressing variability for virtually every diagnosis specific to signs, symptoms, risk factors, patient values, and social determinants of their health … The results of these efforts are clear and positive. Health-services researchers have correlated adherence to evidence-based clinical practices with better outcomes and lower costs. Accreditors and regulators have crafted rules and regulations based on process measures for which hospitals, physicians, and post-acute providers can be held accountable. Government agencies have become more aggressive in scrutinizing quality. And the sweeping change in incen-

tives for providers from volume to value is premised on the assumption that achieving evidence-based thresholds of quality [is] a basis for participating in savings. All these are derivatives of the quality improvement movement in the US system about to begin its third decade.[30]

The disrupters who have powered the quality movement have been challenging the status quo for several decades now—conducting the research, experiments, and measurements that makes progress possible. These disrupters—individuals and institutions—have fueled the reform agenda.

Counter indications notwithstanding, the ubiquity of the decline narrative makes it difficult for many to accept that American health care is on the rise. As Steven Pinker noted, it is not always easy to discern when a historical trend has shifted course. That is precisely why it is so important to step back and look at the broader megatrends in health care, even as it is necessary to lean in and see the improvements spreading from one health system to another. We see it in our own organization as well as in other provider groups throughout the country—ideas for better patient care growing and spreading organically.

In the coming chapters we take the reader on a guided tour of the major trends collectively transforming the US health care-delivery system, including:

- historic breakthroughs in treatments for heart disease, cancer, stroke, and other conditions, thus saving millions of lives;

- integration of behavioral health services into primary care to battle the depression/anxiety epidemic;

---

30   Keckley, "Myth: Quality of Care in US System is the World's Best."

- recognizing and acting upon the broad effect of social determinants of health on large numbers of people and managing the health of populations, especially those with chronic conditions;

- harnessing an astonishing array of technologies—from implantable devices to telehealth;

- identifying new approaches to educating the health care workforce;

- consumer empowerment focused on measures that matter most to patients;

- consolidation of the health care industry along with integration of health services;

- growing quality-reform movement that embodies these trends; and, finally,

- reform of the payment system that has incentivized doctors and hospitals to shift to a newly proactive approach to caring for patients.

Each trend on its own has a certain degree of power, but the greater strength of this movement lies in the interconnectedness of the trends. Shifting to value-based payment, for example, requires a broader view of care delivery, including greater attention to social determinants of health and behavioral health integration in primary care. And treatment breakthroughs along with the technological revolution demand that we educate the health care workforce in a more precise and sustained fashion. Interdependence adds strength and durability to the trends both individually and collectively. Each of these trends is broad and deep enough to merit book-length treatment on their own. We have endeavored in this book to touch

We argue in this book that the nation is at an inflection point that requires acceleration of these trends and that our greatest enemy is the stasis that sometimes grips major stakeholders.

upon the critical points—the highlights, really—in each of these cases.

We argue in this book that the nation is at an inflection point that requires acceleration of these trends and that our greatest enemy is the stasis that sometimes grips major stakeholders. The status quo is too often too comfortable for some health care leaders, yet it is clear that the status quo cannot hold. The industry is changing, and one of the most profound changes involves new ways of paying for care. The health care universe is abuzz with talk about reforming the current payment system—shifting from fee-for-service to value-based payments, which means moving away from the traditional approach of paying for the volume of care to paying for the value of outcomes achieved; it means a shift from being paid for visits, tests, and procedures to being paid to manage a patient's overall health. The fundamental point here is *not about payment* per se, but about new ways of caring for patients that are *a result of* new payment models. We view the term "payment reform" as code language describing the new, proactive method of delivering care.

Listening to the many different players supporting the reform movement, it seems clear that one of the indicators of the shifting landscape is a change in the language of health care. In general, language tends to alter fairly slowly over time, but in this case the evolution of the health care lexicon has accelerated. Not too many years ago, mentions of *value-based care* were rare, and rarer still were debates about *paying for value rather than volume*. At the many conferences held throughout the country these days one hears these terms in virtually every presentation. Dr. Ezekiel J. Emmanuel, health policy expert at the University of Pennsylvania, suggests that this new language is nothing less than "the vocabulary of transformation."[31]

If there is consensus around the megatrend-based reform agenda—and we see plenty of evidence for it—then the next logical question is, How do we get there? The answer, we believe, is clear: the country needs the major players in the health field to join forces in a more sustained movement for change. Progressing to the tipping point will require an effort more strategic than anything that now exists: the joining together of disparate elements into a forceful whole. This requires a focused effort by the most influential players in the industry—physician and hospital groups, employers, consumers, the government, and health plans—to accelerate the megatrend-based reform agenda. There are excellent organizations within the reform movement, but there is a tendency for some groups to work within a silo. More outreach and engagement among these groups could help accelerate evolutionary change. We are not talking here about challenging or skirting antitrust laws, but a collaboration around the goals of reform. Imagine the potential power of these actors—employers, for example, that provide coverage for about half of all working Americans under age sixty-five, (an estimated 178 million people) and the federal government, which regulates the industry while paying the bill for 100 million people. It is important to acknowledge the outsized influence of the federal government within this movement. On one hand, the government's imposition of micromanaged rules and regulations stifles innovation. On the other, the more the government emphasizes the power of the megatrends within the reform

---

31 Emmanuel, *Prescription for the Future.*

agenda, the greater the chances that private payers and providers will do the same. These featured actors, both public and private purchasers of health care, are already ideologically aligned with the reform agenda focused on a mission to keep people healthy.

We consider this book a call-to-action to accelerate the pace of change for the megatrends. We call upon providers, employers, consumers, government regulators, and insurers, as well as elected officials, to take two affirmative steps: First, to recognize the reality on the ground today—that the decline narrative is outdated and that the megatrends are leading US health care in a positive direction. Second, to embrace the reform agenda for the benefit of the health and financial wellbeing of the nation by plunging into the cultural, economic, and political fray and arguing for the megatrend-based agenda. We agree with Ezekiel Emmanuel's view that there now exists "the potential for truly positive, groundbreaking change in the American health care system—more so than at any time" in more than a century, and that innovation "has pushed the American health care system past the tipping point on transformation. The genie is out of the bottle; there is no turning back now."[32]

---

32   Ibid.

CHAPTER TWO

Payment Reform: Bringing Sanity to a Wild-West Marketplace

"Changing the way doctors and hospitals are paid improves the way medicine is practiced and the way patients are treated."

To better understand the essential mechanics of the US health care system, let's consider a highly unusual analogy. Imagine a world in which purchasing an iPhone was similar to purchasing health care. You would buy your phone's component parts from a dozen different suppliers in various locations: flash memory from Samsung, gorilla glass from Corning, mixed signal chips from NXP, touch amplification modules from Skyworks, and so on through numerous additional components. This only seems ridiculous because we know as consumers that we can purchase a fully assembled, fully functional iPhone, and we can do this because Apple knows what the consumer wants and makes sure that is what the consumer gets.

In health care, however, most patients gather the component

parts themselves—making various appointments at different times and places and, eventually, collecting a total experience of care that, in the best cases, results in what the patient actually wants: an overall sense of health and stability. Patients do not set out to engage in a series of shopping adventures for sub-specialists. They would much prefer one-stop shopping, where a product called *health* is provided to them. In many cases in the US today, this product does, in fact, reach the patient, but assembly—clearly more complex with health care than a smartphone—is required. Then there is the issue of cost. Let's say for the sake of discussion that Apple could sell the average iPhone for $400, but that by selling the component parts separately to consumers they could charge $800. In that case, Apple would make the entirely rational economic decision to sell the parts separately and let consumers deal with the assembly challenge. Historically, this is how doctors and hospitals have operated: charge for the component parts of care because it is generally more profitable than not doing so.

As extreme as this example sounds, it fairly accurately represents how health care often works: doctors, hospitals, device makers, pharmaceutical companies, etc., sell component parts of health and too often leave consumers to put the pieces together. Why? Because doctors and hospitals often find themselves boxed into a financial system where they encounter incentives to over-treat patients, prescribe medications, and schedule tests, screenings, and office appointments which may or may not be necessary for a patient's health, but which help support the financial wellbeing of the physician practice and hospital. All of these things are billable events for which the physician group or hospital is compensated by an insurance company, an employer, an individual, or the government.

By no means do we suggest that doctors willfully take actions that are not needed by a patient purely to make money (at least not the vast majority of doctors). The financial reality in medicine is more nuanced. The fee-for-service payment model where doctors and hospitals are paid for the volume of services provided has grown through the years like an invasive species wrapping itself around the care delivery system and choking off payment reform innovation. The result? A world where the default standard is focused on the volume of care rather than the quality of care.

> **The fee-for-service payment model where doctors and hospitals are paid for the volume of services provided has grown through the years like an invasive species wrapping itself around the care delivery system and choking off payment reform innovation.**

There is no perfect model of care delivery—not that we have seen. The good news, however, is that the United States is currently in the midst of one of the most disruptive periods in health care ever, a period in which the country is moving away from the volume-based default setting to proactive health management and paying for value. Though the shift is coming too slowly and needs to be accelerated, it is nonetheless moving in a positive direction. The ultimate goal of value-based payment is to deliver proactive, coordinated, value-based care; to eliminate unnecessary care; and to provide doctors and hospitals with financial incentives to improve quality for patients.

Here is the essence of the matter—when you change the way doctors and hospitals are paid, you change the way doctors practice and the way patients are cared for. For accountants, "payment reform" means a change in how medical care is compensated. For the rest of us—patients, doctors, and those who pay for care—"payment reform" is code language for changing the way doctors practice and the way care

When you change the way doctors and hospitals are paid, you change the way doctors practice and the way patients are cared for.

is delivered. When you read about payment reform in our book, we urge you to think not about dollars, but about how doctors deliver care and how patients receive care. Why the change? Because the people paying for care have reached the end of their rope. The health care purchasing superpowers—major employers and the federal government—have had it up to here.

Based on our own research, nearly six in ten Americans (146 million people) get their health coverage through their employer while another 100 million receive coverage through the government in the form of Medicare and Medicaid. With a combined audience of nearly 250 million people, employers and the government have an unrivaled level of marketplace muscle and those superpowers are now speaking with one voice in saying *enough is enough!* Enough wasted money, time, and treatment; enough with putting doctors in a straitjacket when it comes to flexibility or lack thereof in treating patients; enough with micromanaged regulations by a government insufficiently cognizant of its overreach.

With this unified voice the superpower payers are saying:

We want high-quality, efficient care with minimal waste and delay.

We want doctors to coordinate care for our patients.

We no longer want to pay for volume—for many different tests, procedures, and appointments. Instead, we want to pay for value—*for proactive care toward the overall health of our people.*

Across the country, major health systems are in sync with this approach and are working on the challenging shift from delivering care in a fee-for-service environment to delivering care in a value-based environment. As crazy as it seems, the truth is that traditional payment methods have not been based on the quality of the care delivered to patients. But that is changing.

"We are moving from a world where you get paid to just do more stuff to getting paid because what you did produced a quality outcome," says our colleague Dr. Lawrence Smith, Northwell Health physician-in-chief and dean of the Donald and Barbara Zucker School of Medicine at Hofstra/Northwell. "That is radically different. During my years practicing medicine I got paid the exact same amount if I made a mistake and harmed a patient as if I saved somebody's life. It made no difference. Quality had nothing to do with it."[33]

Now quality is at the heart of the matter. Quality improvement is being driven by all health care stakeholders, including every major provider system in the country. It is being driven by physicians seeking the best care for their patients while earning a reasonable level of compensation, by patients growing more engaged in a partnership with their doctors, and by the payment superpowers who see the pursuit of quality as a way to improve the health of their people while controlling costs. These superpowers possess the financial muscle to change the course of American health care, and that is precisely what they are seeking to do in concert with health systems working along the value-based pathway to improve the health of the population they serve. The change has doctors and hospitals working proactively, reaching out to patients, and delivering evidence-based care that is measured for quality and efficiency. While providers push from

---

33   Charles Kenney, *Disrupting the Status Quo: Northwell Health's Mission to Reshape the Future of Health Care.*

inside the delivery system for value-based care and payment, payers do the same from outside the delivery system. The net result has both providers and payers rowing in the same direction.

One result of this trend has been the creation of various structures where teams collaborate to provide care (Accountable Care Organizations, Patient-Centered Medical Homes, etc.). The ideal includes a personal relationship where care team members anticipate patient needs and make sure that all important tests and screenings are administered in a timely fashion based on the patient's age, gender, and medical condition. In these relationships, a medical team stays on top of making sure that every woman has her mammogram on time every time, that every patient has their colonoscopy on time every time, that every patient with a chronic illness has the medication and care needed to remain healthy. This approach identifies populations of patients with various ailments, particularly high-cost chronic conditions. Through proactive health management including the right preventive measures as well as timely tests and visits, patients achieve a sense of health and wellbeing. Have we achieved this ideal in the US? Not even close. But there has been meaningful progress, and the megatrends we write about, if accelerated, will move the nation steadily closer to this ideal.

And moving forward is important for many reasons, not the least of which is that the current payment system shortchanges hospitals and physician groups. As payment methods evolve one reality does not change: major payers—Medicare, Medicaid, as well as commercial insurance companies—are relentlessly driving down the amount of money they reimburse doctors and hospitals for care. Most major hospital and physician groups are forced to accept Medicare and Medicaid payments that fall short of what it actually costs to provide the right care at the right time in the right setting. And, based on our own experience at Northwell, while commercial insurers pay more reasonable rates they also deny payment in anywhere from 20 to 50 percent of cases. As a result, provider organizations such as ours are forced to spend tens of millions of dollars on appeals to obtain a reasonable payment for the patient care we deliver.

At our own health system, we employ hundreds of people who work exclusively on persuading, cajoling—and in many cases suing—insurance companies to get the money we are owed. Commercial insurance companies, in fact, rely upon these denials to build their own profitability. The major insurers in the United States enjoy substantial rates of profitability—margins that are an order of magnitude greater than anything most providers could ever imagine reaching. While there are providers in certain dominant market conditions earning substantial margins, the reality for most of us on the provider side is that our margins are a fraction of what major insurers, pharma, and device makers enjoy. The shift to value-based payment is no panacea, but, if done thoughtfully and well, it has the potential of paying provider groups more reasonable rates to care for populations of patients while delivering better outcomes.

One of the most important players in the movement toward proactive care management is the Pacific Business Group on Health (PBGH) where Bill Kramer, the group's executive director for national health policy, is a leader in the movement to improve quality and reduce costs. Educated at Harvard and Stanford, Kramer spent more than twenty years as a senior executive at Kaiser Permanente. Kramer notes that an example of how much progress has been made comes in the form of a program in which large employers including Boeing, Pacific Gas & Electric, and the California Public Employees Retirement System (CalPERS) "began working directly with providers to implement a care-management initiative called the Intensive Outpatient Care Program (IOCP)." Kramer told us that the companies "recognized that a high percentage of claims were incurred by a handful of people, and they identified them as people with multiple chronic conditions whose care was not being coordinated well." The program worked so well that the federal government gave a grant "to expand the program to 23 delivery systems providing care to over 15,000 Medicare beneficiaries in five states."[34]

Kramer's colleague David Lansky, president and CEO of the Pacific Business Group on Health, explained that the Intensive Outpatient Care Program "identified 15,000 people with multiple chronic conditions and severe challenges in getting good care, and helped pay for primary care teams that would deliver coordinated care, address social needs, and address mental health needs, all under a prospective payment to the care team." Boeing, PG&E, and CalPERS sought partnerships with provider groups willing to "embrace a different and more proactive model of care which would be primary care-based and would focus on managing patients' chronic conditions more effectively," Kramer explained. The result: reduced hospitalizations and costs.[35]

Many of the targeted patients had conditions that would deteriorate to the point where, on a regular basis, they wound up in the emergency department or were admitted to the hospital. This is the red line defining the relative health of an individual. Patients whose chronic conditions are not well-controlled make frequent use of the emergency department and require admission to the hospital. Patients whose conditions are well controlled are able to avoid both the emergency room and admission to the hospital. Use of the emergency

---

34   Kramer, op. cit.
35   From the NEJM Catalyst event, "Navigating Payment Reform for Providers, Payers, and Pharma," held at Harvard Business School, November 2, 2017.; Kramer, op. cit.

department and admission to the hospital are also the red line on cost: using one or both means very expensive care; avoiding both means better control of costs.

The IOCP "embeds care coordinators in physician practices, where coordinators teach medically complex patients how to manage their conditions and seek to provide seamless transitions among multiple providers and services." (Less assembly required!) The program was based on the premise that if the team could help control the patient's conditions the need for hospital stays would be minimized.[36]

This approach reduced the cost of care for medically complex patients by as much as 20 percent while reducing emergency department visits by half. It demonstrated that "high-risk Medicare beneficiaries treated [within the program] experienced decreases in hospital admissions, inpatient days, and emergency room visits" as well as "health status improvements across a number of areas—patient activation, mental health, and physical functioning."[37]

David Lansky observes that "changing payment, whether in primary care or in hospital care, can make a big difference in the outcomes we're getting."[38]

T his sort of proactive health management is proliferating throughout the country. Three thousand miles away from the Pacific Business Group on Health innovations, Dr. John Hsu and colleagues at Massachusetts General Hospital in Boston initiated their own proactive health-management program. Dr. Hsu wanted to better understand whether participation in a care-management program would help keep patients healthy enough to avoid both visits to the emergency department and inpatient hospitalizations, and whether

---

36 Kramer, op. cit.

37 Ibid.

38 NEJM Catalyst event, op. cit.

such a program might also control the cost of care. Hsu and colleagues compared two groups: one group of patients was enrolled in a care management initiative in which doctors and other clinical team members provided proactive care while the other group was comprised of similar types of patients not enrolled in the care management plan. The result: a 6 percent reduction in emergency department visits, an 8 percent reduction in patients being hospitalized, and a cut in Medicare spending—not a reduction in the rate of increase—but an actual cut in Medicare spending of 6 percent.[39]

A few miles from Mass General Hospital, there exists an ongoing experiment in how to shift from fee-for-service to value-based payment. Over 75 percent of the revenue from Atrius Health's 720,000 patients is pooled into risk-based contracts. (This contrasts with the average physician practice where 29 percent of revenue comes from sources other than fee-for-service).[40]

Under these risk-based arrangements Atrius Health takes responsibility for covering all health care costs for its patients. At one end of the spectrum, there are young, healthy people who require minimal or no care over the course of a year. At the other end of the spectrum are older patients with multiple diseases—diabetes, congestive heart failure, asthma, cancer—all manner of issues. These latter patients are more expensive for the health care system, and the more the patients' conditions deteriorate, the more money it costs. Atrius Health's budgets are adjusted based on the patient's risk level. Since Atrius Health is responsible for the total budget for these patients, there is a significant incentive for Atrius to do all it can as an organization to keep patients' conditions as well-controlled as possible. The

---

39 John Hsu, et al., "Bending the Spending Curve by Altering Care Delivery Patterns: The Role of Care Management Within a Pioneer ACO."

40 Haefner, "Seventy-One Percent of Physicians Practice Revenue Tied to Fee-for-Service in 2016."

incentive to keep people healthy is aligned with the financial interests of Atrius Health; that is, by investing money in ways to keep people well and out of the emergency department and inpatient settings, it costs Atrius Health less overall to care for patients. "We have a very strong incentive to be efficient and have high quality in managing those patients," Dr. Rick Lopez of Atrius Health told us.[41]

Atrius is an example of what is possible more broadly across the US. In risk-based contracts, Lopez explained, "better financial performance comes from reducing unnecessary hospital admissions, using generic drugs instead of brand names, and by providing care in the least expensive high-quality location." Since 2008, Atrius Health has operated on the same Electronic Health Record. Over that time the practice has accumulated a huge amount of patient data. One result of the data warehouse is the ability of doctors to establish registries of patients by category—all patients, for example, who have hypertension or heart failure. "By having and reviewing registries we are able to know who those patients are who need the most help and to track whether we are managing their care gaps," Lopez told us. "If not, we identify those gaps and develop systematic ways to close them." This might mean reaching out to patients and bringing them in for an appointment or for certain treatments. It might mean a change in medication or even a house call by a staff member.[42]

Data helps Atrius doctors identify patients at high risk for hospitalizations and high medical expenses. With this information doctors are able to better manage these patients' conditions and mitigate the risks of hospitalization. Lopez has noticed over the past number of years that quality scores have improved among all the major provider organizations in the Atrius Health greater Boston region. Everyone,

41   Rick Lopez, interview with author.
42   Ibid.

he says, is performing better on quality which means the bar is continually being raised. "We have absolutely improved the quality of our care," Lopez affirms, "and we see that this is industry-wide—everybody is improving steadily across a spectrum of measures, and that means new quality benchmarks are set every few years, and the new benchmarks are always higher."[43]

In our own system here at Northwell Health, Dr. Kris Smith and his colleagues created a program focused on frail, elderly patients suffering from multiple chronic advanced illnesses. To care for them in the best way possible, Smith told us, it is necessary to visit these patients in their homes to both treat them and work with them face-to-face to create a care program that serves their individual needs. "With this program we bring care to patients rather than patients having to come to us," Smith told us. "And we respond to these patients and their families when they need help, not when it is convenient for the health care system to respond. That means same-day visits, availability by phone twenty-four-seven, and home visits by doctors, nurses and paramedics."[44]

This house calls initiative focused on about one thousand and nine hundred elderly patients who struggled leaving home for regular medical appointments. Similar to the situation with the proactive programs we discuss above, this was also a situation in which patients' conditions were not well-controlled and, as a result, they often needed care in the emergency department or as an inpatient. "The functional impairment and medical complexity means these patients wind up in emergency rooms at high rates," says Smith. "Since they cannot get to traditional outpatient care we bring the care to them."[45]

The initiative at Northwell is part of a Medicare demonstration

---

43   Ibid.
44   Kris Smith, interview with author.
45   Ibid.

project called Independence at Home, and the most recent available data show that at Northwell Dr. Smith and his team have succeeded in meeting the six quality goals of the program while, at the same time, reducing the overall cost of care for these patients by 23 percent. The bottom line here is that providing care at home for complex patients makes for a far better patient experience, better medicine, and lower costs. What was particularly notable about this work was that Dr. Smith and colleagues reduced use of the emergency department by these patients by 77 percent and reduced inpatient stays by 53 percent.

"If you can respond to patients in a timely manner," says Smith, "they won't go to the Emergency Department, because no 80-year-old and family wants to spend half the day in the ER getting evaluated for something that can be well-handled at home."[46]

This shift from hospital-based care to ambulatory care is a powerful trend throughout the US, and the adoption of more value-based care serves to accelerate the trend. To keep people healthy, caregivers recognize the need to go to where patients are—in their homes and communities. Within our own system here at Northwell we have experienced a dramatic expansion from 70 percent inpatient, 30 percent ambulatory, just a few years ago to nearly fifty-fifty in 2018.

While the Independence at Home program has been a success, it is clear that no one has found the magic bullet; no one that we are aware of has found the ideal way to deliver care in our country. Health care in the US is not a system so much as it is a series of experiments—a constant state of flux where professionals are trying new ways to improve and deliver care. Many experiments in health care founder, but a number of the new approaches, while imperfect, have proven to work well. The Intensive Outpatient Care Program involving Pacific Business Group on Health, PG&E, Boeing, and CalPERS, demon-

---

46   Ibid.

> **Healthcare in the US is not a system so much as it is a series of experiments—a constant state of flux where professionals are trying new ways to improve and deliver care.**

strates improved quality for patients and improved affordability. The same is true of the primary care initiatives at Mass General, Atrius Health, and at Northwell Health. These programs provide a new pathway going forward. They are, individually and together, a sharp contradiction to the decline narrative.

There is a tidiness to these anecdotes that may mask the difficulty of the work. We do not mean to imply with these examples that the work required of physicians and other caregivers is easy. It is a challenge to make the cultural adaptations needed for doctors and hospitals to transition from one payment method to another, for what they are actually doing is *transitioning from one way of caring for patients to another.* Most doctors were trained during the fee-for-service, pay-for-volume era. Most were also trained under the traditional wait-for-sick-patients-to-arrive care model versus the more proactive approach. Doctors and hospitals have invested billions in data analytics and personnel to be able to care for patients in the more proactive fashion demanded under value-based contracts.

Dr. Patrick Conway, who ran the federal government program overseeing the shift toward paying for value rather than volume, cites areas of marked progress. Under Medicare in 2012, he notes that "we had 0% of payments in alternative-payment models, where the providers were accountable for quality and total cost of care, and by 2016, we were ahead of schedule with over 30% of payment in alternative payment models like accountable care organizations, bundled payments, comprehensive primary care." He cites, as well, widespread progress with bundled payments for orthopedic surgeries. "JAMA studies are showing improved quality at lower cost," he notes.[47]

Dr. Toby Cosgrove, former CEO of the Cleveland Clinic, observes that shifting "from paying for volume to paying for value will require a 'total restructuring'" of the health care industry. "This is an enormous transition," he says. "We've been at it now nine years, and we're just beginning to see the effects of this."[48]

The shift in the tectonic plates requires fundamental changes in the way doctors and hospitals do business, and throughout the country tens of billions of dollars are going toward embracing the new approach. Health care provider groups are investing in advanced-technology systems which enable them to track and analyze patient groups in a way that helps doctors care for them more efficiently to both manage their conditions and keep patients as close to healthy as possible. Physician groups and hospitals are investing not only in information technology to manage and analyze massive stores of data, but also in the kinds of actuarial services traditionally the province of insurance companies.

Imagine for a moment that you are an employer paying for the many hip and knee replacement surgeries your employees need each year. Let's say, for the sake of discussion, that you are responsible for purchasing care on behalf of a large West Coast corporation. You begin by looking around at prices and find that costs for joint replacement surgery in California range from $12,000 to $75,000. Same surgical procedure, wildly different pricing. You also discover that the costs for other high-volume procedures vary widely as well: from $1,000 to

---

47   David Cutler, "The Highest Quality at a Lower Cost? We Don't Have That Yet."
48   Coutré, "Cleveland Clinic CEO Sees 'Total Restructuring' Ahead for Health-Care Business."

$6,500 for cataract removal, from $1,000 to $15,000 for arthroscopy of the knee. Needless to say, you are surprised by these numbers and are wondering how it could be that a straightforward knee procedure could cost *fifteen times more* at one location than another. Could it be that the price discrepancy is due to quality? Is it possible that doctors in one location are fifteen times more competent than doctors across town or that patient outcomes are more than fifteen times better in one place than another? You realize that only in the upside-down world of health care economics could this remotely make any sense. For comparison purposes, let's go back to our offbeat iPhone analogy. Imagine a Verizon store selling an iPhone for $200 and a Sprint store a block away selling the identical phone for $2,000. It would never happen because the iPhone, like the vast majority of consumer products, exists within generally rational economic environs.

While many innovative programs focus on primary care, employers have also pushed for improvements in specialty care, and in that space, again, CalPERS is an innovator. CalPERS spends $7 billion annually covering its retirees and their families, making it one of the largest purchasers of care in the country. In an effort to inject a dose of rationality into the California marketplace for joint-replacement surgery, CalPERS uses its purchasing power to encourage doctors and hospitals to compete on quality and price. CalPERS told hospitals and doctors: *We will pay no more than $30,000* (the original price in 2011). This was the "reference price" for a bundle of care which included all of the pre- and post-op services needed for the particular surgery as well as the surgery itself, all the doctors involved, and the hospital stay. The bundle price was about "the median or some other mid-point in the distribution of prices in the local market." Patients choosing hospitals at or below the designated CalPERS price paid a standard deductible, while patients selecting higher-priced institutions paid as much as $10,000 out-of-pocket.[49]

Health economist Austin Frakt observed in the *New York Times* that "the results of knee and hip replacement surgery reference pricing were striking, as were those for cataract removal, arthroscopy. and colonoscopy." A series of studies found that, as Frakt put it, "under reference pricing, CalPERS patients flocked to lower-priced hospitals and outpatient surgical centers. Prices and total spending for the procedures plummeted." Overall, Frakt wrote, CalPERS achieved a decrease in reference price services of 20 percent even as "typical health care prices paid by employer-sponsored plans rose by about 5.5 percent." Similar bundles of care have grown in popularity and are some of the most successful applications of value-based contracting— i.e., paying for the value of an episode of care rather than the volume of care provided.[50]

Large employers have sought to determine whether there were particular medical centers in the US, not just in California, providing measurably high-quality care at a price below what the most expensive hospitals charged. The answer? Absolutely. Working with Pacific Business Group on Health, these organizations launched the Employers Centers of Excellence Network "which helps employers identify quality providers and negotiate bundled payments."[51]

A select few network medical centers provide employees of participating companies total joint replacements as well as spine care and bariatric surgery. The Centers of Excellence group keeps track

---

49   Boynton and Robinson, "Appropriate Use of Reference Pricing Can Increase Value."

50   Frakt, "How Common Procedures Became 20 Percent Cheaper for Many Californians."

51   Jonathan R. Slotkin et al., "Why GE, Boeing, Lowe's, and Walmart Are Directly Buying Healthcare for Employees," *Harvard Business Review*, June 08, 2017, https://hbr.org/2017/06/why-ge-boeing-lowes-and-walmart-are-directly-buying-healthcare-for-employees.

of quality measures at both the health-center and physician level. To be included in the program, the hospital and doctor must do a high volume of the surgery in question with excellent quality outcomes including overall patient experience of care, functional status ninety days after surgery, and more. The metrics led the team to four medical centers for hip and knee replacements (Johns Hopkins Bayview Medical Center in Baltimore, Maryland; Kaiser Permanente Orange County Irvine Medical Center in Irvine, California; Mercy Hospital in Springfield, Missouri; and Virginia Mason Medical Center in Seattle, Washington) and three medical centers for surgery on the spine (Geisinger Medical Center in Danville, Pennsylvania; Mercy Hospital in Springfield, Missouri; and Virginia Mason Medical Center in Seattle, Washington).

The deal employers offered their workers was simple: if you have your surgery done at one of the Centers of Excellence, *all* expenses will be covered—the cost of surgery and all medical bills (including coverage of the deductible and coinsurance) as well as travel expenses for the patient and a companion. Those choosing to have their surgery at another facility—local, regional, or national medical center—and not one of the Centers of Excellence—would be responsible for the standard deductible and coinsurance, which could run to thousands of dollars. While this approach is hardly widespread in the US, it nonetheless shows promise. As Bill Kramer put it: "Even when factoring in travel expenses and other costs, bundled payments for surgical procedures performed by the Centers of Excellence hospitals cost considerably less than" what these employers had been paying. And on quality measures, the Center of Excellence hospitals were miles ahead of the hospitals not chosen for the elite group.[52]

Just 1 percent of patients treated at a Center of Excellence facility

---

52   Kramer, op. cit.

had to return to the hospital after surgery for additional care. Six times that number had to return to the hospital after surgery at other hospitals. None of the patients operated on at Center of Excellence hospitals required post-surgical stays at a nursing facility while 9 percent of patients at other hospitals required post-surgical care. Bill Kramer told us that the analysis at PBGH found that not only are patient outcomes improved by these bundles, but costs run as much as 15 percent below what would normally be charged under fee-for-service.[53]

Among the most revealing—and in many respects, disturbing—findings from the PBGH study involved the question of *appropriateness*—that is, whether the patient actually needed the recommended surgery. Evidence-based care means just that—delivering care based on scientific evidence that such care is appropriate. And when evidence was applied there were a fair number of patients who were told at the local level that they needed surgery who actually did not.[54]

"While nearly all ... spine patients who presented to one of the participating centers had been recommended for surgery by providers in their home markets, only 62% of the patients were found to be suitable candidates for surgery" by the Center of Excellence hospitals. Put another way, nearly 40% of patients who were told they needed an operation on their spine did not need that operation. Think of the stress, anxiety, and painful recovery process these patients were spared when evidence-based medicine was applied to their cases.[55]

"Instead of unnecessary surgery, activity-based therapies, pain injections, physical therapy, or weight loss were recommended [for the patients] ... Avoiding unnecessary surgery is a significant driver of the program's long-term benefits."[56]

---

53 Ibid.
54 Ibid.
55 Ibid.
56 Ibid.

Orthopedic medicine is not the only specialty area where there is unsettling news about diagnostic mistakes. David Lansky from PBGH reported on a situation where "one of Pacific Business Group's members began a second-opinion cancer service with a world-class cancer center and found that 40 percent of patients who received a second opinion either had, for their first opinion, a wrong diagnosis, wrong staging, or wrong care plan."[57]

The bundle approach has proven to be a relatively successful way to pay for value rather than volume. This is in contrast to pay-for-performance programs built on traditional fee-for-service models that seek to reward doctors and hospitals for quality and efficiency. Austin Frakt and Ashish Jha have noted that the results of such programs have generally been "disappointing." They note, in contrast, that bundled payment programs "represent meaningful departures from the fee-for-service model and its perverse incentives. By encouraging providers to innovate in care delivery within an episode (under bundled payments) or across populations … these programs provide more of the right incentives to improve efficiency."[58]

Let's turn to the other health care superpower, the government. While not known as either particularly innovative or nimble, the federal government, in fact, plays a pivotal role in the transformation from paying for volume to paying for proactive care management. When we talk about the federal government we mean the Centers for Medicare & Medicaid Services (CMS), the department which administers Medicare. In recent years, Medicare has tied more of its payments to the ability of doctors and hospitals to shift from tradi-

---

57 Cutler, "The Highest Quality at a Lower Cost? We Don't Have That Yet."
58 Frakt, and Jha, "Face the Facts: We Need to Change the Way We Do Pay for Performance."

tional payment and traditional ways of treating patients to proactive care management and paying for value. In 2016, 29 percent of health care payments "were made through alternative payment models" including "shared savings, shared risk, bundled payments, or population-based payments."[59]

A key component in the shift is the federal MACRA program (Medicare Access and CHIP Reauthorization Act of 2015), which replaces traditional volume-based, fee-for-service payments with a new set of financial incentives intended to reward doctors and hospitals for improving quality and controlling cost.

"In 2016 payment change was finally moving beyond the experimental phase," wrote Ezekiel Emmanuel, a physician at the University of Pennsylvania. "It was real. It was no longer a matter of if the system would change; the change was happening, and with the passage of MACRA, it moved beyond the point of no return."[60]

MACRA changes the way the federal government pays doctors, which, as we have noted, changes the way doctors care for patients. The most rational actors in any economy do whatever it is they are paid to do. If you are a doctor and you are paid to conduct many different exams and tests, then it is likely you will conduct many different exams and tests. If you fail to do that your value as an employee declines along with your level of compensation. Historically, as we have noted, doctors were paid—and often still are paid—based on the volume of services they provide. Under MACRA, Medicare pays physicians based on their performance on quality, efficiency, improvement of their clinical practice, and use of electronic health-record technology. Medicare has a number of alternative-payment programs

59 "US Healthcare System Ties 29 Percent of Payments to Alternative Payment Models," *Markets Insider,*

60 Emmanuel, op. cit.

all with the same high-quality/lower-cost goal. As of 2017, more than 350,000 clinicians were participating in these alternative-payment models caring for more than twelve million Medicare and Medicaid beneficiaries in all fifty states.[61]

Unfortunately, the evolution to the new payment models—and thereby the new ways of caring for people's health—lacks the dynamic speed needed. The pace of change is not as rapid as it needs to be if the country is going to put the decline narrative fully in the past.

"The industry is going *way* too slowly" in shifting toward value-based payments, observes Leemore Dafny, PhD, a professor at Harvard Business School. "Why? Well, providers aren't completely convinced that buyers (both payers and employers) want change, payers don't want to move without prodding from buyers, and most pharmaceutical industry players are fighting change every step of the way. What is going to speed this up? Budgetary concerns. As cost-sharing increases, consumers are asking why they are paying so much out of pocket *and* in premiums? And providers are frustrated on behalf of patients who can't afford needed medications or visits, not to mention the bad debt arising from high deductibles and co-payments."[62]

Dafny compares the payment reform movement in the US to a stage drama whose gripping opening scene is the Affordable Care Act in which "twelve million [people are] newly enrolled in Medicaid. Ten million signing up for private health insurance plans through the exchanges. Eighty percent of them reporting that they're satisfied with their plans. For a number junkie like me, that's completely gripping. That's the opening. That's why everyone's watching this play. And the

61 Centers for Medicare & Medicaid Services, "New Participants Join Several CMS Alternative Payment Models."
62 Dafny, *Payment Reform is a Play We're All Watching.*

spellbinding finale is supposed to be a completely different way of delivering and receiving health care and maintaining health in this country." But after this riveting opening scene, Dafny says, the show goes sideways.[63]

"This act that we're talking about now—navigating payment reform—it isn't the gripping opening," she says, "or the spellbinding finale." It is an energy drop in the drama where the players seem afflicted with some sort of malaise; where the drama loses its edge. Dafny worries that too many major payers are failing to infuse their roles in the show with sufficient energy.[64]

"We need organizations that are in the field who engage; who don't just sit and watch it happen—because if they don't, that gripping opening could be repealed and we might never even see our fantastic finale," she says.[65]

David Lansky echoes that sentiment. The approaches "we think can work are simply not being adopted fast enough. Instead … employers are beginning" to do it themselves—that is, contracting directly with provider organizations to accelerate the move toward value-based payments and value-based-care delivery. Lansky's view is that the "fantastic finale" Dafny describes may have to come at the insistence of the purchasers of care.[66]

"Purchasers now feel that waiting for the medical professions, the payers, the government, the regulators to solve this problem simply isn't working," Dafny says. "Purchasers are going to need to grab this by the horns and take a leadership position."[67]

Bill Kramer's view is that government plays a critically important

---

63   Ibid.
64   Ibid.
65   Ibid.
66   Lansky, op. cit.
67   Dafny, op. cit.

role in reform, not only for the direct impact on Medicare, but also because the signals that government sends to doctors and hospitals influence the extent to which providers shift to a more proactive form of delivering care.

"It's important to get a critical mass of purchasers insisting on value-based payments, and Medicare is the key," he says. "If Medicare is embracing the move to value-based payments it sends a strong signal to the provider community, and they will get on board. But if Medicare is sending mixed signals it means providers will be slow to embrace alternative-payment models."[68]

Like many other major health systems, at Northwell we are pushing toward value-based delivery of care, but we also recognize that to get too far in front of the trend toward payment shifts could be financially hazardous. In a sense, provider organizations like ours have one foot on the dock and the other in the boat. We would like to be fully in the payment- and delivery-reform boat, and we believe that is where we are headed, but we need payers to accelerate the evolution of payment reform.

We have discussed only a few of the value-based models in this chapter. Even so, the innovations we have covered serve as a substantive contradiction to the decline narrative. The work by CalPERS, the Pacific Business Group on Health, Boeing, PG&E, and others as well as the proactive care programs at Mass General, Atrius Health, and here at Northwell Health are indicators of the progress possible when health care stakeholders are determined to innovate. In the US, all of the major stakeholders in health care are working to improve quality and affordability. As we noted earlier, the delivery system in the US is fragmented, sometimes dysfunctional, and nearly always complex, but amid the turbulence of change there are clear indicators

---

68 Kramer, op. cit.

of improvement in quality and affordability. Not across the board, certainly, but in enough places, tested and measured well enough so that we can say with confidence that in crucial areas of innovation the US is on a productive path.

CHAPTER THREE

Medical Advances:
Miracles of Science

"Blessed to live in such a time."

Among the many different ways to measure scientific progress perhaps the most meaningful is to note that today in the United States millions of people who would have been felled by their diseases just a few decades ago are thriving. This triumph of modern science is a powerful contradiction to the decline narrative. In this chapter we bring you an overview of clinical progress in various areas, including against two of the biggest killers of human beings—cancer and heart disease. We begin on the banks of the Charles River in Cambridge, on the campus of the Massachusetts Institute of Technology with Professor Emeritus Daniel Kelppner.

Professor Kelppner says he was not dreaming of inventing the Global Positioning Satellite when he "helped invent … an atomic clock that's now at the heart of satellite-based global positioning systems. With basic research, you don't begin to recognize the applications until the discoveries are in hand," he told an MIT periodical.

"In [his] view, basic science is the best thing that mankind pursues."[69]

Basic science research is also known as pure, bench, or fundamental research, and it is focused on exploring an infinite variety of unsolved scientific mysteries. It is pure in the sense that basic researchers are not in pursuit of a specific finding, a cure for a particular disease, for example. Rather, their research is in pursuit of knowledge and a deeper understanding of science. Fortunately, however, basic scientific research not only leads to a deeper understanding of the world around us, it also generates new clinical applications that prolong and save lives.

The United States is rich in institutions and individuals who pursue a wide variety of scientific breakthroughs. The major US universities and research laboratories generate fresh knowledge and understanding on a daily basis. At MIT alone, for example:

> Basic research has led to the discovery of the first human cancer gene; the first experimental confirmation of the existence of the quark; the first chemical synthesis of penicillin; and the discovery of *Prochlorococcus*, the most abundant photosynthetic species on Earth … Consider Nobel Laureate Bob Horvitz, who discovered that there are specific genes that determine cell death. Today this discovery is revealing new therapies to treat cancer, Alzheimer's, and Parkinson's disease. Or consider Janet Conrad, whose investigations of the physics of neutrinos are changing the way we understand matter.[70]

At Northwell Health, in an effort to blend pure and applied or translational research, we have invested more than $1.5 billion in the

---

69 Karagianis, *The Brilliance of Basic Research.*

70 Ibid.

Feinstein Institute, the home to some of the leading researchers in immunology and neuroscience in modern medicine. We have added a significant research capability by creating a partnership with Cold Spring Harbor Laboratory, an iconic research center founded in 1890 that today focuses largely on cancer and neuroscience. Home to eight Nobel laureates in its history, the joint venture with Cold Spring Harbor and Feinstein-Northwell is a powerful engine of discovery. The folks at Cold Spring Harbor Lab describe progress versus cancer this way: "In 40 years we've gone from knowing nothing about how a normal cell became a cancer cell to being able to describe that process in exquisite detail. This is driving changes in how we prevent, diagnose, and treat cancers."[71]

Cold Spring Harbor Lab has been one of the stellar facilities in the world for pure scientific research, but as recently as 2015, as the *New York Times* reported, there was something missing: "Despite the many breakthroughs that have taken place… at Cold Spring Harbor Laboratory, there is one thing that has been lacking: human subjects." The laboratory solved that problem by partnering with us here at Northwell, where we diagnose and treat nearly twenty thousand new cancer patients each year. The blending of pure research from Cold Spring Harbor with the applied or translational research of our scientists focused on finding cures for specific diseases, brings the best of both worlds to patients.[72]

I n his Pulitzer Prize winning book, *The Emperor of All Maladies: A Biography of Cancer*, Siddhartha Mukherjee characterizes scientific progress against the disease:

---

71   Cold Spring Harbor Laboratory, "125 Years: Discoveries that Made a Difference 1890-Now."

72   Hartocollis, "Cold Spring Harbor Lab, Seeking Human Subjects, Teams Up with Hospital System."

Incremental advances can add up to transformative change. In 2005, an avalanche of paper cascading through the scientific literature converged on a remarkably consistent message—the national physiognomy of cancer had subtly but fundamentally changed. The mortality for nearly every major form of cancer—lung, breast, colon, and prostate— had continuously dropped for fifteen straight years. There had been no single drastic turn but rather a steady and powerful attrition: mortality had declined by about 1 percent every year. The rate might sound modest, but its cumulative effect was remarkable: *between 1990 and 2005, the cancer-specific death rate had dropped nearly 15 percent, a decline unprecedented in the history of the disease* [emphasis added]. The empire of cancer was still indubitably vast— more than half a million American men and women died of cancer in 2005—but it was losing power, fraying at its borders.[73]

Until as recently as the 1960s, the only clinical treatment for cancer was surgery. Unless surgeons could excise a tumor before the cancer had spread, there was little hope for the patient. And with non-solid tumor cancers such as lymphoma or leukemia, there was virtually nothing doctors could do.

In the late 1960s and early 1970s, Dr. Vincent DeVita at Yale succeeded in curing patients with Hodgkin's Disease via the use of drugs—the first successful administration of chemotherapy. Around that same time some doctors were using radiation treatments, but the approach was fairly primitive, and the side-effects were often debilitating. Dr. Arnold M. Baskies, a National Cancer Institute-trained

73 Mukherjee, *The Emperor of All Maladies*.

oncologist who specializes in surgical oncology, serves as chair of the American Cancer Society board of directors. Dr. Baskies told us the modern story of cancer: treatments and cures which save and prolong life for tens of millions of people whose cancer, just a few years earlier, would have been fatal. In the middle of the twentieth century the overall survival rate for patients with cancer was barely one in four. As of 2017, the survival rate had climbed to nearly seven in ten. And for breast cancer, one of the most common forms of the disease, the overall survival rate has reached 90 percent.[74]

Then, in 1993, came a tipping point: the human genome was decoded, enabling doctors to understand which genes control various diseases. Throughout the world of medicine there exists a palpable sense of excitement about the latest advances in immunotherapy, which Dr. Kevin Tracey of Northwell Health's Feinstein Institute for Medical Research describes as "the ability to use your own white blood cells to kill cancer. White blood cells have the job of killing infections, foreign invaders in the body, but cancer has a way of para-lyzing white blood cells." Cancer turns off the defensive mechanism in these cells, but scientists have now found a way to flip the switch back on so that these cells fight cancer effectively. Immunotherapy is now an option for people diagnosed with a variety of cancers of the head, neck, bladder, lungs, and more. In some cases, immunotherapy can block advanced, late-stage cancers.[75]

The National Cancer Institute defines targeted cancer therapies as "drugs or other substances that block the growth and spread of cancer by interfering with specific molecules … that are involved in the growth, progression, and spread of cancer." These targeted therapies "act on specific molecular targets that are associated with

74   Baskies, interview with author.
75   Tracey, interview with author.

cancer, whereas most standard chemotherapies act on all rapidly dividing normal and cancerous cells."[76]

At present, some patients have cancer that is well-suited for targeted therapy; many others do not. Scientists, however, are working feverishly to increase the numbers and types of cancers that targeted therapies can address. To date, targeted therapies have been approved for treatment of a wide array of cancers, including those of the stomach, bladder, brain, breast, cervix, bones, kidneys, liver, lungs, and more.

Dr. DeVita of Yale has "seen the war on cancer from every possible angle: as a researcher and clinician at the National Cancer Institute, as the longest-serving director of the NCI, as physician in chief at Memorial Sloan Kettering Cancer Center, as director of Yale University's Cancer Center, as president of the American Cancer Society, and … as a patient."[77]

Dr. DeVita declares that in the war on cancer, "we are winning." He notes that by 1990 "the overall incidence of all kinds of cancers in the United States began to decline, as did the overall mortality rates. These figures have continued to decline every year since they peaked in 1990. By 2005 the absolute number of people in the United States who died of cancer declined even as the population was growing and aging (the risk of cancer is higher in the elderly)." Dr. DeVita notes that a number of cancers are "almost completely curable" and that "mortality for certain cancers has declined sharply"—breast cancer by 25 percent and colon cancer by 40 percent. For patients, he says, "the experience of having cancer is also entirely different. The brutal, disfiguring surgeries of the past have given way to less invasive operations, targeted radiation, and new drug therapies." As he looks ahead

---

76   National Cancer Institute, "Targeted Cancer Therapies."

77   DeVita Jr. and DeVita-Raeburn, The Death of Cancer.

Dr. DeVita predicts that "we will see the end of cancer as a major public-health issue. And we have the critical mass of knowledge to get us the rest of the way ..."[78]

Progress is everywhere. The *New York Times* reported that:

> Something strange is going on in medicine. Major diseases, like colon cancer, dementia and heart disease, are waning in wealthy countries, and improved diagnosis and treatment cannot fully explain it. Scientists marvel at this good news ... [I]t looks as if people in the United States and some other wealthy countries are, unexpectedly, starting to beat back the diseases of aging. The leading killers are still the leading killers—cancer, heart disease, stroke—but they are occurring later in life, and people in general are living longer in good health ... since the early 1990s there has been a plunge in colon cancer deaths.[79]

Similar good news comes in reduced rates of hip fractures and even dementia.

As impressive as the advances against cancer are, the progress in treating heart disease is perhaps the greatest medical advance in recent decades. Dr. Steven Nissen, chairman of cardiovascular medicine at the Cleveland Clinic, told us that in the late 1970s, when he was an intern, there was painfully little that could be done for people with heart attacks. "Back then when a patient had a heart attack," he told us, "we would put them in a cool dark place, give them lidocaine and morphine, and hope they didn't die." Now, patients are rushed to the cath lab where doctors perform a series of

---

78 Ibid.
79 Kolata, "A Medical Mystery of the Best Kind: Major Diseases Are in Decline."

once unimaginable steps. A narrow catheter is inserted into a small incision in the patient's groin or neck, and a dye reveals x-ray images of arterial blockages. These blockages, which result from the buildup of plaques along the artery wall, were once fatal. Now, however, when detected, doctors send a miniscule balloon through the artery attached to the end of a catheter. They inflate the balloon, which opens the artery and allows blood to flow freely. The passage is kept open by the insertion—again, through the catheter—of an expandable mesh stent which reinforces the artery walls.[80]

> **"The progress we have made treating heart disease is one of the great triumphs of modern medicine. The age-adjusted mortality rate for cardiac disease has been reduced by about 50 percent. It has been an amazing run."**

"The difference between what we did then and what we do now is just unbelievable," Dr. Nissen told us. "The progress we have made treating heart disease is one of the great triumphs of modern medicine. The age-adjusted mortality rate for cardiac disease has been reduced by about 50 percent. It has been an amazing run."[81]

A crucial moment in the fight against heart disease came in 1987 when research found that newly developed statin drugs lowered bad (LDL) cholesterol so dramatically that it reduced morbidity and mortality and made, in Dr. Nissan's words, "an absolutely incredible difference." Simultaneously, sustained public-health initiatives helped drive down the percentage of people smoking cigarettes from about half the population to about 16 percent. Add to these two advances the development of drugs to control high blood pressure, enabling

---

80   Steven Nissen, interview with author.
81   Ibid.

doctors to normalize pressure in the vast majority of people with hypertension—a development with a "huge impact on heart attack and stroke," says Dr. Nissen. "These advances have allowed heart failure to be a manageable chronic disease as opposed to [a] highly lethal disorder," he continues. From 2000 to 2012, the US achieved more than a 30 percent decline in the death rates for heart disease. Important strides have also been made in the production of drugs to treat congestive heart failure, one of the leading causes of hospitalizations in the US.[82]

As recently as the late 1990s, patients were routinely subjected to chest-cracking bypass surgery to repair heart valves. Now, with the production of progressively miniaturized surgical instruments, that surgery can be done with needle-thin catheters through minute surgical incisions. Additional advances have come from devices such as pacemakers and implantable defibrillators.

Dr. David Brown, a cardiologist, has observed:

> In the 1960s the chance of dying in the days immediately after a heart attack was 30 to 40 percent. In 1975, it was 27 percent. In 1984, it was 19 percent. In 1994, it was about 10 percent. Today, it's about 6 percent … The evolution of heart-attack treatment over the past three decades is a story of doing more things to more people at greater expense with better results. It is a portrait in miniature of medicine in the United States. Although inappropriate care, high administrative costs, inflated prices, and fraud all add to the country's gigantic medical bill, the biggest driver of the upward curve of health spending has been the discovery of new and better things to do when someone gets sick.[83]

---

82   Ibid.
83   Brown, "As Healthcare Quality Rises, So Does Price."

Rosemary Stevens, emeritus professor at the University of Pennsylvania, nicely defines the progress: "The heart is no longer a mystery but a pump with chambers throbbing away from birth to death, serviced by pipes that sometimes get clogged. A diagnosis of heart disease is no longer a death sentence. Problems can be fixed. Not all of them, but many. We are blessed to live in such a time."[84]

There is much more work that needs to be done to defeat heart disease, and perhaps the most pressing issue involves the obesity/diabetes epidemic in America. While clinical teams have improved proactive care for patients with diabetes, there has been little headway on the obesity problem. Too many Americans remain stuck to unhealthy diets and a sedentary lifestyle which conspire to produce cardiac disease. While there are challenges such as obesity, there are also tantalizing opportunities. Scientists are working toward using stem cells to possibly regenerate heart tissue. Being able to repair diseased heart muscle with healthy tissue would be an enormous leap forward. Also, on or just over the horizon are new treatments for high cholesterol—a drug called "PSCK9 inhibitor."

Dr. Nissen has pointed out that "currently, the best available drugs for reducing cholesterol, statins, have been shown to lower the risk of heart attack or stroke up to 35 percent," while "PSCK9 inhibitors have been shown to reduce bad [cholesterol] by as much as 50 percent to 70 percent and demonstrated few, if any, adverse effects."[85]

Consider this as one small measure of progress versus heart disease: at the American Heart Association meeting in the fall of 2017, cardiac experts from around the world presented five thousand scientific papers in a single meeting—most reporting advances in

---

84 Frye, *Caring for the Heart: Mayo Clinic and the Rise of Specialization.*
85 Nissen, op. cit.

knowledge or treatment or both.

Coincidentally, around the same time as the Heart Association meeting, scientists unveiled a way to edit DNA so that diseased genes may be replaced by healthy ones. CRISPR (Clustered Regularly Interspaced Short Palindromic Repeats) enables scientists to remove and replace or alter a piece of DNA.

The New Yorker reported:

> CRISPR has two components. The first is essentially a cellular scalpel that cuts DNA. The other consists of RNA, the molecule most often used to transmit biological information throughout the genome. It serves as a guide, leading the scalpel on a search past thousands of genes until it finds and fixes itself to the precise string of nucleotides it needs to cut. It has been clear at least since Louis Pasteur did some of his earliest experiments into the germ theory of disease, in the nineteenth century, that the immune systems of humans and other vertebrates are capable of adapting to new threats. But few scientists had considered the possibility that single bacterial cells could defend themselves in the same way.[86]

Scientists have used it to edit the genes in sheep and vegetables, but the true promise of CRISPR is to enable scientists to edit genes in order to destroy cancer cells.

Is immunotherapy the Holy Grail for which scientists have been searching for generations? It is too early to tell, but the level of excitement about it throughout the scientific community is undeniable. Already, immunotherapy has saved countless lives, and as scientists work to refine the technique there is the promise of saving thousands, perhaps millions, more lives from cancer.

---

86 Specter, "The Gene Hackers."

Nessan Bermingham, CEO of Intellia Therapeutics Inc. observes:

Looking ahead, [CRISPR] has the potential to drive truly personalized medicine. Medicine has not yet adapted to the genomics revolution that has taken place in the last two decades. What has been missing is a better tool to allow us to interrogate the genomic data and act on it to elicit a therapeutic effect. [CRISPR] is the first viable tool not only to enable us to explore and interrogate the genome but also to provide us with the drug to repair the genome in diseases where limited treatment options are available for patients today. One can envision a time in the not-too-distant future when a patient presents with a genetic disease. Her genome is sequenced, and a genome-editing drug is custom made, targeting her specific mutation. The patient is subsequently treated and potentially cured, in a cost-effective manner. The [CRISPR] technology has the potential to drive a medical revolution in the near future.[87]

Dr. David Shaywitz put it this way:

> "This feels like an unbelievable, almost magical time in bio-pharma—a colleague described it (in a good way) as science fiction coming to life."

This feels like an unbelievable, almost magical time in bio-pharma—a colleague described it (in a good way) as science fiction coming to life. Biological technologies, approaches, and ambitions that might have been dismissed as fantasies only a few years ago now are part of the fabric of the

---

87 Bermingham, Bosley, and Kulkarni, "Realizing the Potential of CRISPR."

industry—and increasingly, it seems, clinical care. Gene therapy, gene editing, cell therapy, immune modulation—these modalities, alone and in combination, are what many in and around biopharma are contemplating, and the sorts of programs many drug-development organizations are hoping to prosecute.[88]

Other areas of medicine have also experienced breakthrough advances:

Premature Infants

It is a miracle of modern medicine that a baby born sixteen weeks prematurely—that is a baby born at just twenty-four weeks—can survive. Babies this premature might weigh no more than a pound and a half. Not so many years ago survival at this stage of development was unheard of, but advances in medicine have given life to countless premature infants. Advances in treatments for immature lungs have come from a particular class of drugs (surfactants), while doctors have also found ways of providing continuous positive airway pressure and other ventilation strategies that increase the ability of a premature infant to survive and grow.

There are effective new treatments to prevent major long-term complications in premature babies including pulmonary hypertension. New hypothermia strategies effectively cool the baby to protect its brain while more precise handling of babies in terms of body temperature and ventilation lowers the risk of hemorrhage. As reported by NICU Awareness:

---

88 Shaywitz, "At J.P. Morgan, A Sense that the Long-Promised Biotech Future Has Arrived; Is Tech Disruption Next?"

The increase of technology to care for premature infants as well as an increase in professional knowledge about premature infants gave hope to babies who in previous decades may have been considered lost causes. Babies as young as twenty-three weeks gestational age and as small as 500 grams were successfully treated. Improvements in nutrition management and new technology allowing for precise fluid delivery, the maintenance of temperature, and proper ventilation management all contributed to helping these very small infants survive. Care has continued to improve, and the survival rate for babies born at twenty-three weeks gestational age is now at 33%; babies born at twenty-four weeks have a survival rate of about 65%. Survival without any major health complications has also increased. These increases show hope for premature babies and their parents, and trends indicate that survival rates will rise even more in coming years. With increasing technology and awareness, survival for premature and sick infants is slowly turning from an exception into the standard."[89]

Orthopedics

Dr. David Battinelli, dean for medical education at the Donald and Barbara Zucker School of Medicine at Hofstra/Northwell, observes that as recently as the late 1990s, it was common to see people—especially older people—hobbling along with the use of a cane. But other than those used for balance, canes have all but disappeared. The reason of course is that when people have pain and restricted mobility due to a defective knee or hip, they get a new one! Advances

---

89 Payne, "A Brief History of Advances in Neonatal Care."

in orthopedics have improved the quality of life for millions. People who, only a few years ago, would have been forced to live in pain with limited mobility, now get new knees and hips and, increasingly, new shoulders and even in some cases new ankles.[90]

Surgical improvements include reduced use of general anesthesia thanks to regional blocks. And the implant devices themselves are considerably more durable than those of an earlier generation—generally lasting a minimum of twenty years. Another area of orthopedics, spine surgery, has also made significant advances. Doctors can surgically correct a curved spine and successfully fuse disks to relieve pain and improve mobility.

Stroke

Just as "time is muscle" in the case of a heart attack, so, too, "time is brain" in the case of a stroke. In an ischemic stroke, oxygen doesn't get to the brain and tissue dies, thus causing paralysis on one side of the body or the other. In this modern era, clot busters such as tPA (tissue plasminogen activator) solve some strokes when administered within four hours of onset.

Increasingly, major medical centers throughout the United States are pushing their stroke center capabilities out to smaller hospitals closer to where people live, thus improving chances of limiting stroke damage. This spreading of medical facilities capable of treating strokes effectively is a critically important advance. Dr. Kevin Sheth, chief of neurocritical care and emergency neurology at Yale School of Medicine, puts it this way:

> Decades ago, when neurologists saw a stroke patient, their job was simply to 'diagnose and say adios,' as it was put then.

---

90   David Battinelli, interview with author.

Today, with new medicines, including those that treat high blood pressure, we have made great strides in stroke prevention. And neurologists like me have new acute treatment options—because research has made them available. As a result, in the past 15 years, stroke has dropped from [number three] to [number five] as a cause of death in the United States.[91]

Bioelectronic Medicine

Another area of progress involves a brilliant new innovation from one of our own physicians—Dr. Kevin Tracey, a neurosurgeon and leader of our Feinstein Institute for Medical Research. In the mid-1990s, Dr. Tracey discovered that a brief electrical impulse applied to a particular nerve could shrink swelling and reduce inflammation. The approach was tested on a group of patients with crippling rheumatoid arthritis. Dr. Tracey wrote about some of the patients in the first round of testing:

> Consider the case of a burly, 47-year-old truck driver from Mostar, Bosnia. Mr. Ostovich has suffered from long-standing rheumatoid arthritis and needed near-permanent bed rest. With his hands and wrists swollen and aching, he could no longer hold on to a wheel or even play with his small children. He tried a variety of medications. None worked. When I met him at his doctor's office in 2012, however, he didn't seem at all afflicted with the disease. That's because, one year earlier, he had been offered the opportunity to be the first participant in a clinical trial of a new therapy based on my invention. He received a bioelectronic implant and

---

91 Sheth, "Too Many People Die from Strokes Because Treatment Is Delayed."

rapidly improved. His mobility restored, he was soon back at work and even … playing tennis.[92]

Then there was the case of Mirela, age thirty-eight, who was written about in the *New York Times*. She had been diagnosed with rheumatoid arthritis at age twenty-two and had "tried nine different medications, including two she had to self-inject. Some of them helped but had nasty side effects." The *Times* story noted that before being treated with the electrical pulse conceived by Tracey, "she could barely grasp a pencil; now she's riding her bicycle to the Dutch coast, a near-20-mile round trip from her home." She told the *Times*: "After the implant, I started to do things I hadn't done in years—like taking long walks or just putting clothes on in the morning without help. I was ecstatic … I got my life back."[93]

Delivering the electrical impulses is a relatively simple matter. The *Times* described the process this way:

> The subjects in the trial each underwent a 45-minute operation. A neurosurgeon fixed an inch-long device shaped like a corkscrew to the vagus nerve on the left side of the neck, and then embedded just below the collarbone a silver-dollar-size "pulse generator" that contained a battery and microprocessor programmed to discharge mild shocks from two electrodes. A thin wire made of a platinum alloy connected the two components beneath the skin. Once the implant was turned on, its preprogrammed charge … zapped the vagus nerve in 60-second bursts, up to four times a day. Typically, a patient's throat felt constricted and tingly for a moment. After a week or two, arthritic pain began to

---

92 Kenney, op. it.
93 Behar, "Can the Nervous System be Hacked?"

subside. Swollen joints shrank, and blood tests that checked for inflammatory markers usually showed striking declines.[94]

Since 1998, Dr. Tracey and his colleagues have published a series of papers in various journals, including *Science* and *Nature*, which demonstrate, as Tracey puts it, "the validity of using electrons to replace drugs."[95]

A paper Tracey published in *Nature* in 2000 reporting his research into bioelectronic medicine has been cited thousands of times, and his work has been written about in the *Times*, the *Wall Street Journal*, and other publications, and he was invited to write the cover article in *Scientific American*. The potential is such that private investors as well as major pharmaceutical companies have invested hundreds of millions of dollars to further develop bioelectronic medicine. No wonder. Tracey believes that it has promise far beyond rheumatoid arthritis:

> There is very interesting data that diabetes can be modulated or potentially treated through nerve signals, so that is a major target. Cancer is another. Although this is several years from clinical development, the opportunity to do the research is now. For example, there is already evidence in cancer that neurotransmitters and nerve signaling can control tumor cell growth and metastasis. Moreover, autoimmune disease, rheumatoid arthritis, inflammatory bowel disease, Crohn's disease, and psoriasis are on the list of potential targets, because the immunology mechanisms of these syndromes is where we started, and we know what to do. Hypertension is a major target. There are 1 billion hypertensive patients on

---

94   Ibid.
95   Tracy, op. cit.

the planet, and despite the available medications, millions of patients are inadequately treated. Compliance is terrible.[96]

He notes that drugs that in some cases cost tens of thousands of dollars per year are not effective in all patients and may carry "black-box warnings, which means that death is a possible side effect." Why would patients pursue a drug regimen when they could opt for a few electronic pulses? Is it possible that treatments like this, pulses through electronic devices, could replace some drugs in the coming years as preferred treatments? Tracey believes it is, and that is perhaps why the pharmaceutical industry closely follows his work.[97]

"The potential of this is so staggering," says Dr. Lawrence Smith. "I don't think anyone knows yet how far this can go."[98]

We asked a number of our doctors here at Northwell to highlight important advances in their respective fields, and what follows is a sample of what we heard. Some of these innovations improve existing processes, while others are wholly inventive and create brand new ways of treating patients. In all of these cases, however, it is clear that an innovative spirit, long a core characteristic of American medicine, is as strong and perhaps even stronger than ever.

It is clear that an innovative spirit, long a core characteristic of American medicine, is as strong and perhaps even stronger than ever.

---

96   Ibid.
97   Ibid.
98   Kenney, op. cit.

Medical Advances

CARDIOLOGY

- percutaneous aortic valve replacement for aortic stenosis

- use of fractional flow reserve to determine significance of coronary lesions, invasive measurements, and CT-FFR (fractional flow reserve-computed tomography)

- development of newer stents that allow early discontinuation of antiplatelet agents

- new techniques to open chronically occluded coronary arteries

- use of radial artery to perform invasive coronary procedures to reduce bleeding and improve survival

- use of left ventricular assist devices to support patients in shock or severe heart failure

CARDIOVASCULAR AND THORACIC SURGERY

- structural heart-disease procedures including transcatheter aortic valve replacement and the addition of transcatheter mitral valve replacement and repair

- LVAD (left ventricular assist device) and ecmo (extracorporeal membrane oxygenation) to support playing a more dominant role in the treatment of advanced heart failure

- robotic thoracic surgery and robotic mitral and single vessel bypass procedures

- heart-in-a-box revolutionizing heart transplantation

- targeted cytokine and small molecule inhibition for the management of inflammatory skin conditions including psoriasis, atopic dermatitis, and hidradenitis suppurativa

- propranolol for the management of infantile hemangiomas

- neoadjuvant therapy for locally advanced basal cell carcinoma with a small molecule inhibitor

- molecular targeted therapy and immunotherapy for metastatic melanoma

- reflectance confocal microscopy for in vivo, non-invasive imaging of melanoma involving the epidermis and the superficial papillary dermis

- discovery of the Merkel cell polyomavirus and its clonal integration in approximately 80 percent of Merkel cell carcinomas

EMERGENCY MEDICINE

- free standing emergency departments

- SBIRT (Screening Brief Intervention and Referral to Treatment) program for vulnerable patients in the ED

- tele-health programs (tele-psych, stroke, and E-ICU) for the ED

- resuscitation (improved CPR, faster defibrillation, therapeutic hypothermia, telephone-dispatcher-assisted CPR instruction, and high-performance resuscitation teams)

- ultrasound for abdominal, cardiac, ob-gyn, trauma, and extremity related pathology in the ED

- sepsis care (early goal-directed sepsis care, sepsis bundle care)

- EMS care of patients (home EMS visits, improved EMS community response time)

FAMILY MEDICINE

- treatment and cure of hepatitis C in the primary care setting

- the use of point-of-care ultrasound in the family physician's office

- telemedicine to augment access for patients and when using consults

- primary care medical genomics, interpretation, and utilization of medical genomics testing to manage patients in the primary care setting

NEUROLOGY

- Autoimmune disorders of brain and neuroimmunology: discovery of rapidly emerging spectrum of autoimmune encephalitis caused by anti-neuronal cell surface and synaptic proteins and their link to neuropsychiatric disorders such as psychosis and depression; these disorders are not that uncommon and often life-threatening. Despite the devastating nature of these illnesses, they are often completely reversible

- newer immune modulatory treatments for inflammatory demyelinating disorders

- epilepsy: newer treatments of drug-resistant epilepsy including neurostimulation (such as responsive neurostimulation system or RNS), in addition to resective surgery

- stroke: cutting-edge technologies (e.g., mechanical throm-bectomy) for management of ischemic large-vessel stroke, including endovascular approach

NEUROSURGERY

- endovascular treatment of brain aneurysms, AVMs (arte-riovenous malformations) stroke and various other cere-brovascular disorders

- radiosurgery: focused conformal radiation delivered via a gamma knife (or similar device) to treat tumors and vascular lesions in the brain without a surgical incision

- deep brain stimulation for the treatment of movement disorders such as Parkinson's disease and essential tremors, with numerous other potential applications being explored (such as depression, obsessive compulsive disorder, anorexia, etc.).

- brain machine interface: using brain waves recorded via an implanted microsensor to perform tasks in a paralyzed limb via external stimulation

- vagal nerve stimulation for the treatment of rheumatoid arthritis

OBSTETRICS AND GYNECOLOGY

- NIPS (noninvasive prenatal screening): currently methods exist to extract fetal DNA from maternal blood sample. This then allows calculating the likelihood of fetal chro-mosomal abn (Trisomy 21, 18, 13). The sensitivity of this screening test is over 99 percent. NIPS has resulted in a significant drop in invasive procedures and, as a result, a drop in pregnancy losses.

- minimally invasive surgery (including robotic surgery): currently the majority of gynecologic surgeries (including gyn oncology) are performed by minimally invasive technique (laparoscopy/robotic). This has resulted in faster recovery, better outcomes, fewer hospitalizations.

- BRCA testing for family members of women with Breast/Ovarian cancer: currently for these first-degree relatives that test positive for the BRCA gene prophylactic surgery/close follow up are the best methods to decrease their lifelong risk for developing cancer.

- IVF (in vitro fertilization): IVF allows women who could never conceive in the past (fallopian tube issues, ovarian issues etc.) to conceive and carry to term. In addition, this method is now used to screen embryos from couples where both are carriers of abnormal genes. In these cases, prior to transfer, the analysis of the embryo allows us to transfer only those embryos with a normal genetic makeup.

OCCUPATIONAL MEDICINE, EPIDEMIOLOGY, AND PREVENTION

- wide ranging health impacts from a man-made disaster— the World Trade Center—and its impact on hundreds of thousands of individuals

- impact of climate change on humans with examples such as influx of dengue to countries farther north than previously reported

- impact of the changing workplace on human health

OPHTHALMOLOGY

- anti-VEGF therapy (anti-vascular endothelial growth factor) for wet "macular degeneration"

- endothelial keratoplasty for cornea transplantation

- sutureless cataract surgery

- laser treatment of many ocular conditions including glaucoma, cataract surgery, retinal disease, refractive surgery

- PROSE (prosthetic replacement of the ocular surface ecosystem) scleral contact lens therapy for cornea ectasia and ocular surface disease

ORTHOPEDIC SURGERY

- complex, minimally invasive arthroscopic surgery and joint reconstruction of especially the shoulder and hip

- robotic surgery and spine, hip, and knee replacement, including material, minimally invasive approaches and pain management advances contributing to limited-stay procedures

- cartilage transplantation for joint injuries

- extremity, digit, and hand surgical replant and transplant procedures

- limb-salvage orthopedic oncology treatment advances and treatment of bone tumors

OTOLARYNGOLOGY

- laparoscopically harvested microvascular omental flap for head and neck reconstruction

- super-selective intra-arterial Cetuximab with or without radiation for recurrent unresectable head and neck cancer

- an implantable sphenopalatine ganglion neurostimulator for the management of chronic cluster headache

PATHOLOGY

- next-generation sequencing for genetics and genomics

- massive-scale multiplex analysis of genetic sequence variations

- digital pathology

- bioinformatics analytics ("big data")

- targeted therapeutics

PEDIATRICS

- enhanced newborn screening for genetic disease (partially discovered here at Northwell's Cohen's Children's Medical Center)

- new vaccines (especially for Hemophilus influenza)

- artificial surfactant for newborn respiratory distress syndrome

- CART (chimeric antigen receptor) cells for leukemia treatment

- genetic diagnostic techniques including WES (whole exome sequencing) and WGS (whole genome sequencing)

- epidural stimulation to restore voluntary movement after spinal cord injury

- robotic therapy as an effective treatment for motor recovery after stroke

- the rapid incorporation of musculoskeletal ultrasound as a diagnostic and therapeutic tool in musculoskeletal medicine

- intrathecal baclofen treatment as an effective treatment for generalized spasticity after spinal-cord injury, traumatic brain injury, and other central nervous system disorders

- intramuscular botulinum toxin as an effective treatment for regional spasticity of limbs and bladder after spinal cord injury, traumatic brain injury, and other central nervous system disorders

PSYCHIATRY

- Longitudinal MRI study finding progressive structural brain changes occurring from the earliest phases of psychotic illness; nature of pathological processes underlying these progressive changes remains unclear but may reflect anomalies of synaptic plasticity, abnormal brain maturation, the adverse effects of stress, or other environmental factors.

- comprehensive versus usual community care for first-episode psychosis: two-year outcomes from the National Institute of Mental Health, recovery after an initial schizophrenia episode early-treatment program

- largest study of comprehensive specialty care for first episode schizophrenia in US demonstrated feasibility and effectiveness of such an approach in "real-world" community clinics across the US.

- report seven genome-wide significant schizophrenia associations (five of which are new) in a two-stage analysis of 51,695 individuals; also report loci that confer susceptibility to both bipolar disorder and schizophrenia.

RADIOLOGY

- CT Angiography: data acquired from a CT scanner can be reconstructed to create 3D images of blood vessels throughout the body. This has allowed for the non-invasive diagnostic imaging of vasculature throughout the body including peripheral, visceral, coronary, cerebral, and pulmonary veins and arteries.

- combination imaging systems: combination PET-CT and PET-MRI systems have been developed which allow for the near-simultaneous acquisition of anatomic and functional imaging data. This has allowed for extremely accurate localization of metabolic tracers which circulate throughout the body.

- interventional oncology: in recent years, a number of minimally invasive techniques have been developed to treat tumors with extremes of temperature, by interfering with their blood supply, or by delivering targeted chemotherapy. These procedures are performed under imaging guidance.

- neoadjuvant chemotherapy for bladder cancer

- novel immunotherapy for renal cancer

- normothermic perfusion for cadaveric kidneys

- active surveillance for prostate cancer; low risk for prostate cancer; no difference in mortality than radiation or surgery but higher progression of metastasis

- bucal mucosal grafting for ureteral strictures

- shock-wave lithotripsy for erectile dysfunction

This is a partial list. When you drill down into any one of these medical advances you find the purpose of the entire enterprise—patients whose diseases are cured or well-managed, human beings whose sufferings are alleviated. Each item on this list represents innumerable human stories that affirm what it is that we do in health care. We concede to those promoting the decline narrative that the delivery system is imperfect—no question. But we also recognize its strength and effectiveness in healing. While this chapter has focused almost entirely within what is generally considered the strictly medical realm, the next chapter is considerably broader and looks at the social determinates that play such a large role in health. We go, in other words, from inside the doctor's office and hospital in this chapter to outside those walls in the next.

CHAPTER FOUR

Social Determinants: The Power of Zip Code as Well as Genetic Code

"Fresh food as medicine."

magine a scene where you are strolling in the country with two friends and you come upon raging whitewater cascading to a boulder-strewn riverbed. Suddenly, you see children in the water tumbling downstream headed for the falls. You plunge into the water and grab a child, then another, and drag them to shore, and you keep going back into the water and pulling other children out and, while you are doing this, one of your two friends gathers sturdy branches and assembles a raft to save a number of children simultaneously. And then, exhausted from your labors, you see out of the corner of your eye that your other friend is rushing along the riverbank, running upstream *away* from the falls. Incredulous, you call out, asking what's going on, and she replies that she is "going to find out who or what is causing these children to fall into the river—and I'm going to put a stop to it."

This little parable is well-known in the public-health community for obvious reasons, and it is a story that Dr. Rishi Manchanda likes to tell when he is talking about his focus on the upstream issues that affect the health of millions of people in the United States. During his years practicing medicine in Los Angeles, Dr. Manchanda found time and time again that the causes of his patients' medical issues were traceable back upstream to the conditions in which they lived. He explains that one of his patients, Veronica, suffered for a prolonged period from severe headaches. She lived in South Central Los Angeles, and when she was in acute pain she would go to a local emergency department where doctors would examine her, administer tests, and provide her with medication. But the problem persisted over time. When Veronica showed up in Dr. Manchanda's clinic, he asked her about her symptoms, of course, but he also asked her about her living conditions.

Upon investigation, it turned out that her headaches resulted from an allergic reaction to mold in her apartment. Dr. Manchanda prescribed some medicine for her pain but he also gave her an unusual prescription that called for a visit to her home by a community health worker capable of identifying and eliminating threats to Veronica's health—mold, for example. And, if need be, the doctor told her, he could provide her with an additional prescription for a public-interest attorney in the event that her landlord wasn't providing the appropriate level of safe, hygienic housing required by law.

Dr. Manchanda has become a leading evangelist for "upstreamism"; the belief that effective medical care requires an understanding of the social circumstances that influence a person's health, such as safe housing, fresh food, transportation, employment, etc. He details his thinking on the topic in his book, *The Upstream Doctors*.

"Medicine can do better when it works to improve health where it begins—in the social and environmental conditions that make people sick," he says. "Why treat people only to send them back to the conditions that made them sick in the first place?" He argues that "zip code matters more than genetic code when it comes to health outcomes."[99]

The circumstances in which we live and what we eat, etc., "have more than five times the impact on our health outcomes than all the … pills and procedures the doctors prescribe."[100]

This trend is so powerful that working to address the social determinants of health has become a priority for virtually every major health care organization in the country. Kaiser Permanente's Rachel Gold states that "the growing awareness of the importance of [social determinants of health] is changing how health care is delivered at Kaiser Permanente … and around the nation."[101]

Steven Pinker cites the classic upstreamist, public-health example in his book *Enlightenment Now: The Case for Reason, Science, Humanism, and Progress.* He writes that "before the 20th century, cities were piled high in excrement, their rivers and lakes viscous with waste, and their residents drinking and washing their clothes in putrid brown liquid. Epidemics were blamed on miasmas—foul-smelling air—until John Snow (1813–1858), the first epidemiologist, determined that cholera-stricken Londoners got their water from an intake pipe that was downstream from an outflow of sewage."[102]

This trend toward greater awareness of the social determinants of health is one of the most encouraging developments in health care, for it creates a greater awareness among providers of the whole patient, including all of the various elements—most of them outside what might be considered strictly medical issues—that effect an individual's

---

99   Manchanda and Roz, "How Can Your Home Make You Sick?"
100 Ibid.
101 Gold, "Addressing Social Needs to Improve Health at Kaiser Permanente and Beyond.
102 Pinker, *Enlightenment Now.*

overall health and wellbeing. The US Centers for Disease Control and Prevention defines the *social determinants of health* as "economic and social conditions that influence the health of people and communities. These conditions are shaped by the amount of money, power, and resources that people have, all of which are influenced by policy choices … Factors related to health outcomes include" everything from "how a person develops during the first few years of life" to "what kind of work a person does" to whether a person has social support.[103]

More precisely, according to the organization HealthBegins, "scientists generally recognize five determinants of health of a population:" (1) a person's genetic makeup; (2) personal behaviors such as drug or alcohol use; (3) the social environment in which a person lives—whether there is discrimination in housing, employment, or education; (4) the physical environment in which a person lives—whether it is dangerous, has open parkland, etc.; and (5) the availability of medical care.[104]

Education, employment, level of income, marriage stability, access to transportation, and good nutrition are all associated with overall health and wellbeing. The importance of the social determinants has long been recognized particularly in the public health arena, but it is only in recent years that there has been significant focus in this area by physicians and others delivering care at the front lines. Only recently has there been a general awareness in medicine that all of these social factors dwarf the impact of medical interventions in terms of general health. Consider the amount of time a person spends in the doctor's office. Even someone with multiple chronic conditions is likely to be in a medical practice clinic no more than ten to twenty

---

103 US Centers for Disease Control and Prevention, "About Social Determinants of health."
104 HealthBegins, "Overview."

hours a year. The vast majority of their time people are at home, work, or school, and it is the conditions in these places that play a central role in determining an individual's health.

"Let's say you spend twenty-four hours a year in the doctor's office—one full day," posits our Northwell colleague Dr. Mark Jarrett. "Your health is largely determined by what happens the other 364 days of the year." Put another way—health care is only one of many components of health.[105]

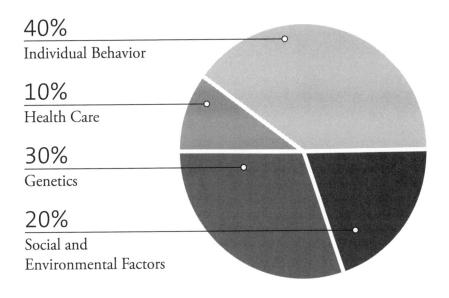

40%
Individual Behavior

10%
Health Care

30%
Genetics

20%
Social and
Environmental Factors

Source: *New England Journal of Medicine*

Commentary from the University of Utah helps put the determinants of health into perspective.

We've vaccinated billions of babies, invented penicillin, developed an artificial heart, and mapped the human

105 Mark Jarrett, interview with author.

genome. But the most significant advancement of public health over the past two hundred years was a government infrastructure project—diverting sewage and wastewater away from drinking-water sources and chlorinating and filtering the water coming out of the tap. Clean water has cut overall mortality in major cities in half and infant deaths by three-fourths. If the most important global health accomplishment ever achieved was through water pipes, where should we be focusing our efforts today? ... Making sure our patients have clean water (think Flint, Michigan) and good schools and fresh vegetables and convenient transportation and adequate housing and a living wage? Should the bulk of our efforts be focused on stopping smoking, conquering obesity, ending addiction, addressing mental health, and tackling poverty? Truly taking care of the community—addressing all the social determinants of health—is perhaps the most disruptive idea that's ever been posed to our health care system.[106]

> "Truly taking care of the community—addressing all the social determinants of health—is perhaps the most disruptive idea that's ever been posed to our health care system."

But where, exactly, do you draw the line? When is the issue more one of social services than medicine? It's one thing for a physician to counsel a patient on how to quit smoking or eat healthier foods, but should a doctor be assigned responsibility for a patient's housing, employment, or neighborhood safety? These items fall well outside the traditional purview of medical doctors,

---

106 University of Utah Health, "Algorithms for Innovation."

nurses, and other caregivers, and doctors justifiably protest that they are already overwhelmed and cannot get into the business of solving society's broader social ills.

That is not to say that doctors are unaware of the effect of social circumstances. In a survey, the Robert Wood Johnson Foundation found that "four out of five physicians believe that a patient's environment plays a large role in his or her illness." The same survey, however, revealed that physicians view most social determinants as well outside their scope of influence and perhaps their scope of responsibility as well.[107]

We do not suggest that physicians should be in the business of accessing housing, employment, or transportation for their patients—certainly not directly. But we do believe that information about a patient's social situation should be in the electronic health record so that a doctor may refer patients to social-service agencies or hand off the case to another member of the health care team, such as a physician's assistant or community health worker. In fact, major insurance companies have issued billing codes (ICD-10 codes) for social determinants.

In the summer of 2018, the federal government took an important step toward recognizing the importance of social determinants. The federal Chronic Care Act enables Medicare to pay for benefits that "can include social and medical services, home improvements like wheelchair ramps, transportation to doctor's offices, and home delivery of hot meals," according to the *New York Times*, which quoted one of the law's authors, Senator Ron Wyden of Oregon, saying that the law "begins a transformational change in the way Medicare works for seniors who suffer from chronic conditions. More of them will be able to receive care at home, so they can stay independent and out of the hospital." The *Times* quoted a former Medicare

---

107 Robert Wood Johnson Foundation, "Health Care's Blind Side."

official as saying that "an inexpensive railing in the bath can avoid a fall that can cause a hip fracture and potential complications."[108]

What, exactly, should doctors and hospital leaders be expected to *do* to effect social determinants of health? Manchanda has a thoughtful response. He calls for health care professionals to work at various levels depending upon the issue—to *lead* on some issues, to *partner* with social-service agencies and perhaps government on other issues, and to *support* broad initiatives that get at the social determinants. Think about the influence of individual doctors—smart, highly educated people who are often among the most influential people in their communities. Hospital leaders—physicians, administrators, trustees—are major employers and thus have significant influence as well. On an issue such as the epidemic of complex chronic conditions plaguing America, it is up to health care professionals to be the leaders working toward solutions. This falls squarely into the physician's purview. On other broader societal issues, Manchanda told us that his message for doctors is to "use your position of power. Lead collaborations; bring people to the table."[109]

On the partnership level, he told us, doctors and hospital leaders might join forces with local agencies such as the YMCA to foster programs that get people together to exercise and perhaps learn about improved nutrition. At the support level, Manchanda says, consider broader societal issues such as the minimum wage or other things that effect poverty and economic insecurity. Think about the major medical centers in a city publicly supporting an initiative to raise the minimum wage or to strengthen environmental regulations concerning air pollution, which affects the asthma suffered by inner-city kids.[110]

---

108 Pear, "Medicare Allows More Benefits for Chronically Ill, Aiming to Improve Care for Millions."

109 Manchanda, and Roz, op. cit.

110 Ibid.

"On the issue of raising the minimum wage, doctors say, 'that's not my job—I'm not a legislator or a politician,'" yet the voices of physician leaders can be quite powerful, he argues.[111]

"We need physicians to lead, partner, or support efforts to move upstream; for example, advocating for food security for people with diabetes," he told us. A doctor "doesn't have to become a transportation expert or a

> **"We need physicians to lead, partner, or support efforts to move upstream."**

mold expert or a social worker, but a doctor should certainly know how to contact a transportation expert or a social worker or a mold expert with the same ease that a doctor can call a cardiologist to take care of that heart murmur."[112]

Here is an example of a physician improving health by reaching way outside the hospital walls: Dr. Jeff Nicastro, an emergency department physician on Staten Island, noticed that every few weeks auto accident victims were showing up in the ER from crashes on the same stretch of Hylan Boulevard. The data confirmed his observations and led to city officials changing traffic signs and lights, resulting in a decrease in accidents in that area.

At the Donald and Barbara Zucker School of Medicine at Hofstra/Northwell, our students are exposed to social determinants from the start of their education when they certify as EMTs. Working on ambulances that respond to every manner of emergency, the students see inside one home after another and in that way come face-to-face with determinants such as poverty, lack of safe and secure housing, insufficient food supply, etc.

An example of partnership and support might be physician and

---

111 Ibid.
112 Ibid.

hospital associations voicing public concern over guns. As we have noted in the past: gun violence isn't just a national tragedy, it's also a public health crisis. At Northwell, we are part of the Greater New York Hospital Association which has come out in support of specific action to curb gun violence. The association's statement noted that members are "dedicated to public-health matters and emergency preparedness [and that] the issue of gun violence is therefore an ever-present concern in what we do. Our primary mission of caregiving is being diluted by our nation's failure to enact meaningful reforms to address the plague of gun violence." In the wake of the horrific murders at various schools throughout the country, the association articulated support for a series of five specific steps:[113]

1. Outlaw assault rifles in all forms that they exist.

2. Enhance background-check requirements and reporting on the National Instant Criminal Background Check System (NICS), and increase the minimum age for gun purchases.

3. Invest substantially more in mental health care and ensure that the most vulnerable among us have access to effective assessment and treatment while recognizing that such investments may have only an incremental effect on prevention.

4. Permit the Centers for Disease Control and Prevention and the National Institutes of Health to conduct research into the causes of and remedies to gun violence, which, unbelievably, is prohibited under current law.

5. Substantially increase awareness and training for the identification of risk factors, along the lines of New York's "see

---

113 Greater New York Hospital Association, "Statement on Gun Violence as Adopted by the Greater New York Hospital Association Executive Committee on March 1, 2018."

something, say something" campaign and pass "red-flag" laws allowing family members to petition the courts for temporary removal of firearms from individuals of concern."

In recent years Dr. Manchanda's upstream focus has come to the point where he has founded an organization—HealthBegins—dedicated to spreading the upstream gospel. HealthBegins is "a think-and-do-tank that demonstrates how a smarter health care system improves health where it begins—where we live, work, eat, learn, and play." The organization helps caregivers do a better job of addressing the social determinants by providing education and training programs.[114]

Dr. Paul Farmer, co-founder of Partners in Health, an organization which cares for poor people in Haiti and other nations, is a strong supporter of Manchanda's work. Dr. Farmer is an iconic figure in medicine who holds a university professorship at Harvard and was the subject of the Pulitzer Prize-winning book *Mountains Beyond Mountains*. In a review of Manchanda's book, *The Upstream Doctors,* Farmer wrote:

> The upstreamist approach is not merely to inquire about the causes of the causes [of illness]; it also calls for addressing them. The clinic in which Dr. Manchanda practiced as an upstreamist works with community health workers and tenants' rights groups, which, in essence, extend the clinic right into their patients' homes (if they have them) and lives. The medical staff connected [Manchanda's patient] Veronica to a community health worker, who could visit her at home and help make sure she was able to obtain and take the medications likely to give her short-term relief from her

114 HealthBegins, op.cit.

symptoms. That's one of the things that community health workers do … As for her housing conditions, another partnership came into play: a tenants' rights advocacy group, long active in Veronica's neighborhood, petitioned the landlord—this time with a doctor's note in hand—to make the improvements that were always part of his contractual agreements and were in keeping with local building codes.[115]

Throughout the country there is a greater understanding than ever before about the importance of social determinants and a growing desire to work back upstream. At Kaiser Permanente, the nation's largest integrated health-delivery system, for example, there is an affirmative effort to "target our members' unmet social needs." Consistent with Manchanda's exhortation for provider organizations to lead, partner, or support, Kaiser Permanente has created a partnership with Health Leads, a social services organization which provides a variety of services to patients.[116]

Working with the guidance of Health Leads, Kaiser teams reach out to the 1 percent of their patients who use the system the most (super-utilizers) and connects these people to a variety of community resources that can help patients with fresh food, housing needs, and more. Health Leads patient advocates work on behalf of super-utilizers throughout the care process from initial clinic appointments to follow-up aimed at ensuring the patient has the medications and appointments needed and also is in touch with whatever community social services are required.[117]

A critical element of the service has Health Leads patient

---

115 Paul Farmer, "Investigating the Root Causes of the Global Health Crisis: Paul Farmer on the TED Book *The Upstream Doctors.*"
116 Gold, op. cit.
117 Shah, et al., "Healthcare that Targets Unmet Social Needs."

advocates communicating directly "with the clinical team, providing frequent updates on the status of patients' progress. This not only enables physicians to work with patients in a way that accounts for the realities of their lives, but also gives the physician a better understanding of the entire patient population."[118]

As we discussed earlier in the book, an essential element within the decline narrative centers on rankings indicating the US lagging behind other nations on life expectancy and other measures. Here is where an interesting discussion comes up comparing what other nations spend on social services versus spending in the US.

It seems fairly clear that other rich nations, particularly in Europe, offer a sturdier safety net for their people in terms of employment, housing, income security, retirement security, and other factors at the heart of the social determinants of health. In the US, we spend far more on health care—on doctors, hospitals, procedures, drugs, etc.—but comparatively less on social services. Here is the intersection where many people believe the US needs to do better. "Research shows that nations that focus on food insecurity, housing, transportation, and other 'nonmedical' factors spend less overall on health care while improving quality and quantity of life."[119]

The trend in the United States toward value-based payments is aligned with the need to go upstream to improve health at the root cause. There is a domino effect here: changing the way you pay doctors means doctors focus more on proactive care, which in turn means going back upstream and targeting social determinants. It is an exciting convergence of three trends in health care: (1) going

---

118 Health Lead, "Kaiser's Center for Total Health Highlights Health Leads as Innovative Healthcare Solution."
119 Shah et al., op. cit.

> **There is a domino effect here: changing the way you pay doctors means doctors focus more on proactive care, which in turn means going back upstream and targeting social determinants.**

upstream, (2) the shift from fee-for-service to paying for value, and (3) managing populations of patients, especially those with multiple chronic conditions.

"Now with value-based care it's imperative to figure this out," Manchanda told us. An indication of the growing awareness of the need to address social determinants is the increasing number of conferences that feature speakers on the topic. More than that, there are now regular gatherings of health care professionals focused entirely on learning how to better work upstream. And Manchanda's organization, HealthBegins, now teaches and offers consulting services to health care organizations on improving their upstream work. The alignment comes down to the simple fact that doctors and hospitals, increasingly, are paid for outcomes rather than procedures. If you are a physician group and you can go back upstream and keep patients healthy it improves patient lives as well as your own financial situation. Some organizations are taking direct action on determinants of health in ways rarely done before. Boston Medical Center, for example, which cares for many poor and homeless people, is partnering with social-service organizations to build housing for those in need.[120]

Getting at the determinants of health frequently means going to the patient's home to make an assessment and deliver care. This is a kind of back-to-the-future of doctors and their black bags making house calls, although now the bag has been supplemented by

---

120 Manchanda and Roz, op. cit.

a smartphone, tablet, or laptop, or a combination of all three.

A good example comes from a *New York Times* report on a program within our own organization. The article, by reporter Paula Span, centers on an eighty-eight-year-old, Mrs. V, who is suffering from dementia, kidney disease, and diabetes. Under this new program paramedics go to Mrs. V's home to provide care in an effort to both improve her health and keep her out of the hospital. For some time, she had been a very frequent visitor to the emergency department, until, that is, the folks from the Northwell Health House Calls program began paying her in-home visits. Out of ten visits to her home by paramedics responding to her calls, she had to be taken to the emergency room only once. "In all the other cases the paramedics were able to solve her problem and make sure she was safe and stable in her home. When Mrs. V falls or seems lethargic or short of breath, her aides no longer call 911," the *Times* reported:[121]

> They dial the House Calls service at Northwell Health [and community paramedics] often arrive in an SUV instead of an ambulance. And with 40 hours of training in addition to the usual paramedic curriculum, they can treat most of [Mrs. V's] problems on the spot instead of bustling her away. 'A lot of what's been done in the ER can safely and effectively be done in the home,' said Karen Abrashkin, an internist with Northwell's House Calls program and [Mrs. V's] primary care physician. For frail, older people with many health problems, Dr. Abrashkin noted, 'the hospital is not always the safest or best place to be.'[122]

The *Times* noted that results from the program published in the

121 Span, "Going to the Emergency Room Without Leaving the Living Room."
122 Ibid.

Journal of the American Geriatrics Society found that in 78 percent of cases paramedics were able to treat frail elderly people in their home and avoid a trip to the hospital. This comprised 1,602 ailing, homebound patients (median age: eighty-three) over sixteen months.[123]

"On each call, the paramedics, acting as physician extenders, consulted with doctors by phone or a secure video link. They performed physical exams and ran electrocardiograms. They treated breathing problems with nebulizers, administered diuretics and oxygen for heart failure symptoms, and provided IV fluids for dehydration."[124]

The question of how major medical centers in the US should target the determinants of health has been the subject of intense discussion during recent years. Like many other organizations, we have struggled with it, sought to find the right approach—the right balance between our traditional healing role and the newly-acknowledged responsibility to do more outside our own walls. And we've made what we think are important steps forward including in the way we think about the communities we serve and the social determinants that effect health. We have benefitted by the addition to our team of Dr. Ram Raju, Northwell's community health investment officer, who previously served as CEO of the New York City Health and Hospitals Corporation, the largest public-health system in the country.

"When a patient comes with chest pain we identify the clinical risk factors," he told us. "We have to add to a patient's profile his or her social risk factors if we are to fully understand the total patient. Where does the patient live, do they have money for food, for prescriptions, is there a park nearby where they can walk each day. We are taking the social risk factors and developing a social vulnerability index so that when a patient comes in the physician sees the full

---

123 Ibid.
124 Ibid.

picture of what effects the patient's health."[125]

Based on these social risk factors our physicians are empowered to refer patients to a variety of social service agencies and programs Perhaps the most important social risk factor—both among our patient population and throughout the nation—involves food. In California, a pilot project includes a "'food as medicine' approach increasingly embraced by physicians, health insurers, researchers, and public health officials."[126]

Within the communities we serve at Northwell, there are an estimated 1.4 million people "who live in a food desert," says Dr. Raju. "Meaning they have no access to fresh food within a five-mile radius. Think of the impact that has on patients with diabetes, for example, who need fresh food to control their blood sugar."[127]

We have come up with what we believe is a solution that will help mitigate the problem for some of our patients. The Northwell Health food as health program allows doctors to write a prescription for fresh food for their patients. Patients take the prescription to an area stocked with fresh foods from Long Island farms and purchase that food. (Many patients receive a financial subsidy as well.) This program, in association with Long Island farmers and the US Department of Agriculture, is up and running in just one of our hospitals as of this writing (summer 2018), but our plan is to expand to sixteen additional hospitals within the next year.

"This is fresh food as medicine," says Dr. Raju. "Food as a source of healing."[128]

---

125 Raju, interview with author.
126 Brown, "Cod and 'Immune Broth': California Tests Food as Medicine."
127 Raju, op. cit.
128 Ibid.

CHAPTER FIVE

Technology: The Age of Smart Medicine

"I have never seen such an acceleration of new technology, both hardware and software, across every dimension of medical practice."

Sean Duffy, the thirty-four-year-old founder and CEO of Omada Health, lives in the expanding landscape at the intersection of technology and medical care. A self-described "computer nerd," Duffy earned a neuroscience degree from Columbia with a plan to become a practicing physician. His passion for technology led him to a stint at Google before joining the Harvard MD/MBA program. While in medical school, however, with a growing understanding of the power of technology, he came to believe that he could help improve the health of many more people as a technology entrepreneur than as a doctor. As he examined various ways of integrating technology more fully into health care, Duffy came to embrace a radical notion: the in-person visit in health care—what is now the first step in many medical encounters—might be someday thought of as a last resort, after first exploring options to safely and effectively resolve a patient's needs remotely.

Duffy explained his thinking in a provocative article he co-authored with Dr. Thomas Lee: "What if health care were designed so that in-person visits were the second, third, or even last option for meeting routine patient needs, rather than the first?" they write. Duffy and Lee observe that "viewing in-person physician visits as a last resort sounds radical, but it just represents a deepened commitment to patient-centered care ..." and a gift of time and convenience for people who do not want life interrupted by travel to a clinic waiting area, crowded with sick people, to see a doctor for fifteen minutes.[129]

In-person visits "will certainly always have a central role in health care [but] ... a system focused on high-quality non-visit care would work better for many." In fact, they note, the approach is already working in the largest private integrated health system in the US. At Kaiser Permanente, 52 percent of "the more than 100 million patient encounters each year are now 'virtual visits,'" via text messages, calls, email, or video conferencing.[130]

We do not want to imply that the shift from in-person to virtual care is easy, and certainly we agree with Duffy and Lee that face-to-face sessions with a doctor will "always have a central role in health care," especially for people with a serious illness. The shift to more virtual visits presents a logistical challenge, of course, but perhaps more than that it is a cultural challenge. At one end of the interaction, patients must be comfortable that they are receiving quality care in a secure, private environment. Adoption of technology in health care can be deeply disruptive. The difficulty that many provider organizations have faced when integrating a new electronic health record,

---

129 Duffy and Lee, "In-Person Healthcare as Option B."
130 Ibid.

for example, is widely known. But with the smartphone, there is no learning curve to speak of. Billions of people worldwide are experts in its use because they rely upon their phone for multiple other uses including communication, banking, travel arrangements, and more. The fact is that many people "live" on their devices—laptop, tablet, and, especially, smartphone. At the other end of the encounter—with the physician—there is comparable expertise in digital devices. This baseline level of comfort with the tools makes the next step—actually connecting online for care—somewhat less daunting.[131]

Duffy believes the new generation of doctors stand especially ready and willing to engage in virtual care delivery. He points to recent and current medical school classes where increasing numbers of students possess deep interest in science along with the power of technology to better treat patients. Growing numbers of students, he notes, come to medical school with degrees not in biology or chemistry but in computer science. "In the next generation of doctors, we'll find many that are deep in technology with an instinct for how tech can solve a variety of problems," he told us.[132]

Technological applications in health care are far from perfect. Exhibit A is the electronic health record (EHR), which has made the blood of countless physicians boil with frustration. The EHR can be a cruel taskmaster, demanding a doctor's attention during a patient visit and requiring numerous clicks to enter even basic data. As one physician put it in the *Wall Street Journal*, the widespread adoption of electronic health records has required "a seismic cultural shift." While this shift has contributed mightily to burnout among physicians, it is also true that with time doctors become more used to these systems

---

131 Ibid.
132 Ibid.

and the systems themselves are revised and adapted (somewhat) to the ways doctors actually practice.[133]

Notwithstanding the challenges with EHRs, the reality today is that in health care, technology is a force of nature. It is important to recognize that there are two distinct categories of technology within health care, and they are progressing at distinctly different rates. There is medical technology in the delivery of care to patients and then there is information technology in interacting with consumers. On the medical care side the technology is the stuff of Star Wars. Some of the most advanced technological tools ever developed in any field are in use to care for patients. Look at any modern operating room or intensive care unit and the technology to treat patients and keep them alive is remarkable. On the IT consumer engagement side, however, the strides to date have been less impressive, but that is changing. While some older physicians have struggled to adopt EHR technologies, younger, tech-savvy medical students and doctors have little trouble with these technologies. And it seems more than likely that with the passage of time a new generation of technically competent and comfortable doctors will remake these records into tools that are easier to use and more patient-centered.

Computers, tablets, sensors, and video monitors are essential tools, but the most powerful technological tool in the health care arsenal may well be a smartphone. It is estimated that there now exist *several hundred thousand* smartphone apps related to health care: apps connected to wearable sensors that calibrate blood pressure, heart

---

133 *Wall Street Journal*, "Doctors Debate Electronic Health Records."

rate, glucose levels, breathing rate, and a variety of other measures that indicate the state of an individual's health. Monitors signal doctors when patients need to be seen, require blood work or other testing, or when their medication needs to be altered. Doctors are eagerly anticipating a breakthrough in natural language processing which would enable physicians to have a computer record their notes while speaking to the patient.

Like Sean Duffy, Dr. Eric Topol of the Scripps Research Institute is deeply tech savvy. Topol's 2015 book, *The Patient Will See You Now*, is among the definitive works on the role of technology in health care. In a review of the book, Dr. David Shaywitz, another tech expert, wrote that "we instinctively reach for our smartphones when we need to take pictures, get directions, deposit checks, or reserve a table. Eric Topol, a cardiologist and digital pioneer, thinks that they are ready to perform at least one more task: revolutionize health care."[134]

Topol writes that the smartphone is "the most rapidly adopted technology in the history of man," and the "hub" of health care's technological revolution. As we have previously noted, the trends we write about are leading health care in a positive direction, but the pace of change is insufficient. So, too, with the adoption of technology in health care delivery.[135]

Topol continues: "We need to move much more aggressively into the era of smart medicine, using high-tech tools to tailor more precise and economical care for individual patients," Topol wrote in the *Wall Street Journal*. He does not minimize the challenge, noting that the transition to a more technology-rich medical environment "won't be easy or fast" in large measure because "the culture of medical practice is famously conservative." But the opportunities are so great,

---

134 Shaywitz, "Doctor Android."
135 Topol, "The Smart-Medicine Solution to the Healthcare Crisis."

he writes, that "in [his] three decades as a doctor, [he has] never seen such an acceleration of new technology, both hardware and software, across every dimension of medical practice ... The new tools are not just more powerful, precise, and convenient; they are more economical, driven by the information revolution's ability to deliver ... ever-increasing computing power for less money."[136]

The use of technologies such as smartphones, tablets, and laptops signals the beginnings of the age of the consumer in health care. In a general sense, as patient, a person is subservient to the provider. As consumer, the person is more empowered with greater access to information and an ability to behave as consumers do in other fields.

The notion of in-person care as a last resort sounds radical to many people but certainly not to the folks at Apple, Google, and other technology companies. Apple, Amazon, Facebook, Google, and Microsoft changed the world; they altered the way people interact with one another, conduct business, purchase products. And all five of these giants, building on their particular strengths, are digging ever deeper into health care. As one venture capitalist observed: "Apple is trying to drag medicine from where it currently takes place—in hospitals and clinics—and move it to the consumer side, to your phone."[137]

To the folks at Apple, the shift to virtual visits is hardly radical at all. In fact, they see it as a perfectly natural next step in the evolution to immersing the smartphone into every aspect of life. Apple's health care ambitions are by no means modest. The company is currently consolidating medical records on the iPhone in partnership with a dozen major medical centers, including Johns Hopkins, Cedars-Sinai, and Geisinger Health System.

---

136 Ibid.
137 Singer, "How Big Tech Is Going After Your Healthcare."

The existing new reality is that a fat file, that until recently was stored away unavailable to the patient, now sits in its entirety on the patient's phone. For patients with chronic conditions who make frequent use of medical services, this leap forward enables them, whether a mile from their doctor's office or a thousand miles, to track and share with their doctor essential data on blood pressure, heart rate, glucose levels, and scores of other important clinical markers. Think about how radically different this is from traditional medical practice. Rather than having a patient come into the clinic for regular checkups, doctors can now receive daily readings from patients who are in their own homes. The amount of information the doctor now has about the patient is an order of magnitude larger than before, and doctors can react in real time to changes in a patient's condition. And all of this is happening on a device with which both patient and care-team members are intimately familiar.

Needless to say, for certain situations, there is no replacement for face-to-face interaction with your doctor—but it doesn't always require a visit to the clinic to make this happen. It can be done—and is being done—via *telehealth*. Dr. John Noseworthy, CEO at the Mayo Clinic, defines telehealth—or telemedicine as Mayo calls it—as "the remote delivery of health care through a secure video or computer link." Telemedicine "delivers the right care, at the right time, and in the right place—whether that place is a patient's home or a distant clinic facility without sub-specialty care resources," he says.[138]

Telehealth technology enables patient and physician in different locations to communicate face-to-face via laptop or smartphone to solve a variety of medical problems. The power of telehealth is the ability to connect the right physician expertise to the patient regardless of where either might be in the physical world.

---

138 Noseworthy, "Telemedicine Will Increase Access to Care, Reduce Costs."

Like Mayo, Northwell Health has been an early adopter of tele-health. The work here has been led by Dr. Marty Doerfler, one of the pioneers in telehealth in the United States. The modern incarnation of telehealth goes back to 1998 when a group of physicians and entrepreneurs at Johns Hopkins started a company called VISICU, where Doerfler served as medical director and VP for clinical services.

"The company was founded after a project with Johns Hopkins critical care physicians [working] from their homes [with] a Johns Hopkins affiliate that did not have round-the-clock critical care physicians like the mother ship did off hours," he told us. "It showed a significant improvement in patient outcomes."[139]

At Northwell, Dr. Doerfler led the creation of a tele-intensive-care unit (eICU®) which has doctors, nurses and advanced clinical practitioners (nurse practitioners and physician assistants) in a central location assisting with care in eleven different ICUs. The program utilizes two-way audio/video technology and a "smart" software built upon a relational database to transmit information from the patient's bedside to experts at a central telehealth unit staffed by intensive-care physicians and critical-care nurses. In the monitoring center Dr. Doerfler's team can watch over multiple patients simultaneously:

> The clinicians at the telehealth center are given real-time access to all of the important patient information that various machines are recording in the patient's room— cardiac rhythms, heart rate, pulse, labs, radiographic images, etc. Every room is wired with high-resolution zoom camera, speaker, microphone and monitor. It is its own ecosystem in each room. The microphones, speakers, and two-way video allow for direct communication between the eICU

---

139 Doerfler, interview with author.

and bedside teams. With the eICU we can do everything I could do if I was on site except touch the patient. Because an intensivist or other bedside ICU staff member can only be in one place at a time, the eICU team can also help the staff in the hospital to keep watch over the entire population of critical care patients. In the intensive care space if the patient has a problem in bed one, and the staff are busy in bed two—they're going to be tied up there for forty-five minutes—by the time they're free bed one has potentially progressed more than they would have otherwise. The patient in bed one's problem by definition is less severe than the individual in bed two, but if you had the ability to be there from a remote site you might improve things.[140]

This level of monitoring is somewhat analogous to air traffic control. "If you go back to the early days of air travel the pilot flew a plane and he or she was in the plane alone," says Doerfler. "Then you progressed to commercial air travel where they had a staff, but it was still the plane being flown exclusively by the people in it. At some point along the way you introduced air traffic control. You had the ability to know what all those planes were doing and communicate between them and give extra assistance to the ones that were landing, or the ones that were traveling through bad weather or experiencing other problems or risks. You were able to leverage a resource to be a part of the travel of every plane in the sky."[141]

This approach in health care enables team members to see the forest for the trees. "If you're looking from above you are not occupied with the things that only people at the bedside can do, such as performing a procedure, and while they are doing those things the remote

---

140 Ibid.
141 Ibid.

team is looking at data, reviewing the chart, looking at the plan again and seeing the new labs coming in." Doerfler has an interesting term he considers something of an oxymoron, which he uses in connection to telehealth: "It's *preventive care in an intensive care environment.* Preventive care is getting your flu shot and your colonoscopy whenever you hit those various ages, but, looking at somebody at two o'clock in the morning in the ICU, you are preventing things that might otherwise go wrong."[142]

At Northwell, as of early 2018, the eICU approach had reduced both hospital and ICU lengths-of-stay and, more importantly, cut severity-adjusted mortality by 30 percent.

I t is perhaps somewhat counterintuitive, but telehealth has proven to work well in treating some psychiatric patients. When we think about psychiatry it typically involves face-to-face encounters, but with the limited availability of psychiatrists in the US, telepsychiatry has become an important option.

"There are no psychiatrists in most emergency departments from Friday at five until Monday at eight," observes Doerfler. "Well, it's Friday night at seven o'clock and you've got a sixteen-year-old in crisis and you're bringing her in for an acute evaluation because she cut herself with a razor blade."[143]

Before the introduction of telehealth visits with a psychiatrist for patients in the emergency department, this particular case could have resulted in the girl being held in the ED over the weekend—an agonizing wait for patient and family. With a secure camera and monitor in the ER, however, a psychiatrist can connect via telehealth to the patient and her family in a matter of minutes. The doctor

---

142 Ibid.
143 Ibid.

interviews the patient and family, makes a diagnosis, prescribes medication if needed, and writes a treatment plan. In the course of doing the telepsych work, Doerfler and his colleagues made a significant discovery related to efficient use of psychiatrists' time. They found that in this type of situation it typically took a psychiatrist about two hours to evaluate the patient and fill in the administrative boxes needed to get the patient admitted.

But it seemed wasteful of the psychiatrist's time to have to cover all of the administrative steps in addition to the virtual meeting with the patient and recommendation for treatment. After looking at the process Doerfler says that team members created a new role they call "behavioral telehealthcare manager" to triage psychiatric patients and manage logistics such as admission and finding a bed. An analysis found that 75 percent of what the psychiatrist had been doing could be done well by the behavioral telehealthcare manager. Thus, rather than a psychiatrist spending nearly two hours per case, they now spend about thirty minutes, thus freeing these doctors to treat many more patients.[144]

As teams at Northwell, and places such as the Mayo and Cleveland Clinics, explore telehealth opportunities, they are simultaneously trying to figure out the potential applications in health care of artificial intelligence (AI). While telehealth is up and running and very real, AI remains in its early stages. But the possibilities are such that there is much excitement about a future in which smart computers require only seconds to make a complex diagnosis and prescribe a treatment plan. The hope and promise of AI is tantalizing, but doctors have varied levels of excitement about it.

Eric Topol is enthusiastic, writing that "algorithms and artificial

---

144 Ibid.

The hope and promise of AI is tantalizing, but doctors have varied levels of excitement about it.

intelligence are making it possible for doctors to rapidly apply relevant medical literature to their patients' cases." He notes that AI advances allow "computers to read as many as 260 million medical scans in a day, at a cost of $1,000."[145]

Dr. Doerfler is less sanguine. "Right now, AI is unable to explain itself," he says. "Humans are not going to trust a machine making a decision until it understands why the machine made the decision."[146]

In general, there has been more hype around AI in health care than meaningful results. The British medical journal *The Lancet* observed:

Demonstrable successes with deep learning in other industries have awoken clinical interest. The resulting partnerships between clinicians and data scientists, supported by growing strength of clinical informatics, are beginning to yield positive results. With this change, the skills required to understand the informatics of large datasets, and the insights that can be drawn from them, have become an essential pillar of clinical practice, alongside evidence-based medicine ... but from the melee, quality collaborative research is emerging. AI requires thorough and systematic evaluation prior to integration in routine clinical care, but, like other disruptive technologies in the past, the potential impact should not be underestimated.[147]

---

145 Topol, op. cit.
146 Topol, op. cit.
147 *The Lancet*, "Artificial Intelligence in Health Care: Within Touching Distance."

Sometimes, the simplest technologies can make a significant difference in patient care. Monitoring the health of older people with chronic conditions once involved video conferencing, but now seniors, from their homes, can stay in touch with their care teams via a simple tablet. With this approach, a nurse, via smartphone, connects with the patient who uses a tablet. They can see one another and converse about whatever issues might have arisen with the patient. This approach, especially when focused on patients at high risk of readmission to the hospital, enables the care team to respond with whatever level of intervention the patient needs from treatment instructions to a home visit. The beauty of the system is that it allows the nurse and patient to have a televisit any time, day or night. Initially, using this approach at Northwell, there was some concern that patients in their eighties or older, for example, might be resistant to using a tablet, but the system is so simple and intuitive that few patients have had trouble adapting. One drawback to this approach is that insurers generally do not pay for this service, which is yet another reason why accelerating the shift to value-based payments makes sense.

Notwithstanding the payment obstacles, the verdict is in on the effectiveness of telehealth visits. In telepsychiatry, for example, at Northwell we achieved an 88 percent reduction in the time it takes to connect a patient with a psychiatrist for a consultation in the emergency department. With our telestroke program, we have reduced door-to-needle time and increased the number of patients receiving tPA. And we have experienced a reduction in mortality rates with eICU.

Having begun this chapter with Sean Duffy, perhaps it is appropriate that we close with him as well. His story from his medical school and Google days is a fascinating one about technology and entrepreneurship, and it has continued since he founded Omada Health in

2011. The company's intensive lifestyle program targets people *at risk* of suffering from chronic conditions—the many millions of patients likely to progress through the chronic-disease continuum.

The company explains on its website that "Omada uses behavioral science grounded in foundational, peer-reviewed literature to help people change their habits, improve their health, and reduce their risk of chronic disease … The Omada program guides participants through an inspiring and interactive journey that integrates seamlessly into everyday life. Every participant is supported by a professional health coach and robust social network for feedback, support, and accountability … Our outcomes-based pricing model means that if the Omada program doesn't work, we're not charging as if it is."[148]

Working through employers, health plans, and health care-delivery systems, Omada has enrolled more than 175,000 participants in its program. Omada uses health-screening questionnaires to "identify and enroll only those individuals who are on the brink of tipping over into certain chronic conditions, including type 2 diabetes and heart disease."[149]

Duffy told us that there have been nine peer-reviewed studies of the Omada approach, which found that "within 12 months the average participant in the program successfully lowers weight to a level that's shown to reduce risk of diabetes by 30 percent, the risk of heart disease by 13 percent, and the risk of stroke by 16 percent."[150]

The Omada program was the subject of a report in the *Wall Street Journal* in June 2017 focused on a collaboration among Omada, the American Heart Association, and Intermountain Healthcare in Salt Lake City:

---

148 Omada Health, "Scientific Games."
149 Ibid.
150 Duffy and Lee, op. cit.

The year-long program starts with a core 16-week online course on better lifestyle habits and assigns patients to a personal health coach and private online support forum with moderated discussions. Participants receive a pedometer and a cellular scale that transmits their weight readings to their Omada profile and are visible to the coach. They log their daily activity and food either online or with a mobile app; if they have a connected device such as an Apple Watch, they can link it with the program to transmit activity automatically. Their results are displayed on a personal dashboard. After the initial sessions, Omada provides a 36-week sustaining curriculum focusing on weight maintenance ... [Participants] are able to maintain weight loss and lower average blood-sugar levels two years after starting. In one study of 501 Humana Medicare Advantage beneficiaries, published in the *Journal of Aging and Health*, participants lost 7.5% of their initial weight after 12 months, improved blood-sugar levels, and lowered cholesterol. In addition to reducing their risk of diabetes, participants also reported improvements in self-care, diet and exercise, and lower feelings of depression and isolation.[151]

---

151 Landro, "How Apps Can Help Manage Chronic Diseases."

CHAPTER SIX

Behavioral Health: Caring for Mind and Body

"Behavioral health integration into primary care is on its way to becoming a new standard of care in the US."

I n 1999, the Surgeon General of the United States made an alarming discovery: fifty million Americans were suffering from mental disorders such as depression and anxiety, but the great majority received no treatment. When Dr. David Satcher convened the first ever White House conference on mental health, he and his colleagues found that "major depression [was] the leading cause of disability" in the US. The combination of the Surgeon General's conference and subsequent report sought "to dispel the myths and stigma surrounding mental illness," and to convey the idea that "mental illnesses are just as real as other illnesses."[152]

Perhaps the most important element of the report was its explicit recognition of the powerful linkage between mental and physical

---

152 *National Health Policy*, "Dispelling the Myths and Stigma of Mental Illness: The Surgeon General's Report on Mental Health."

health. Experts found that in many patients, mental issues exacerbated physical conditions, particularly chronic illnesses. In the 1980s and '90s doctors found that more and more patients with physical issues were also troubled by behavioral concerns—anxiety, depression, obsessive/compulsive behavior, and other mental ailments.[153]

"It's a vicious spiral," observed Dr. Jürgen Unützer of the University of Washington. Unützer's research found that when a patient with diabetes, for example, experienced worsening physical symptoms, he or she would also often experience more acute signs of depression and vice-versa.[154]

Particularly interesting in the Surgeon General's report was the notion that doctors and other mental health professionals had grown increasingly skilled at helping people suffering from mental issues, but that there was a chasm between the professionals and those in need. How could a relative handful of psychiatrists in the US possibly spread out to treat fifty million people?

In Washington, DC, Dr. Satcher didn't have an answer for that, but in Seattle, at the University of Washington, a psychiatrist named Wayne Katon had been working on solving the problem for twenty years. While a resident in the late 1970s, Dr. Katon saw that the great majority of people with anxiety and depression did not get needed treatment. This stood in contrast to the situation with physical medicine where people with physical ailments—a broken leg or ruptured appendix, for example—were treated promptly. Why were people with depression and anxiety essentially ignored or treated as though mental illness is less serious somehow than a physical ailment?

While the stigma surrounding mental health conditions has lessened considerably through the years, it nonetheless remains a signifi-

---

153 Ibid.
154 Aston, "Closing the Behavioral Health Gap Through Collaboration."

cant reason why there is such a gap in the treatment of mental health in the US. Many people are simply too embarrassed to seek treatment for depression and anxiety. The obstacle remains so serious that an increasing number of professionals suggest the use of the term "brain health" rather than "mental health" as a way to reduce the stigma.

Another problem has been the relative isolation of the psychiatric profession. While it was true that psychiatrics went to medical school, their subsequent clinical training was so far removed from other doctors that they tended to live in a psychiatric silo. In many ways psychiatrists had walled themselves off from the rest of the medical profession.

"Behavioral health care is mostly separated from the primary care system—a practice that the Institute of Medicine concluded nearly 20 years ago was leading to inferior care," according to a 2014 report:[155]

> In the intervening years, evidence has continued to mount that having two, mostly independent systems of care leads to worse health outcomes and higher total spending, particularly for patients with comorbid physical and behavioral health conditions ranging from depression and anxiety, which often accompany physical health conditions, to substance abuse and more serious and persistent mental illnesses ... patients with these diagnoses use more medical resources, are more likely to be hospitalized for medical conditions, and are readmitted to the hospital more frequently. This evidence—combined with the growing recognition that physical, mental, and social challenges are interrelated—has led to calls to integrate behavioral health care into primary care services.[156]

---

155 Klein and Hostetter, "Integrating Behavioral Health and Primary Care."
156 Ibid.

> What might be possible if the wall between psychiatrists and doctors treating physical maladies came down? What if, instead of psychiatric care being something apart from the normal practice of medicine, it was available to the great masses of people?

What might be possible if the wall between psychiatrists and doctors treating physical maladies came down? What if, instead of psychiatric care being something apart from the normal practice of medicine, it was available to the great masses of people? And what if you could figure out a way to multiply the psychiatric loaves and fishes, to extend a psychiatrist's involvement with hundreds of patients in a given week, even indirectly? Katon "saw that if we could empower the primary care system to improve the recognition and quality of treatment, we could have a tremendous public health impact, more so than [he] could as a psychiatrist seeing individual patients."[157]

The trick was to figure out a way of integrating behavioral health into a primary care practice without disrupting already stressed primary care operations—no easy task. Primary care doctors, after all, were under tremendous pressure throughout their days juggling one patient after another in sessions that were often severely time-constrained. Initially, many doctors pushed back against integrating behavioral health in primary care. *I am already overwhelmed with work,* doctors said. *I don't have enough time and even if I did I was not trained in this.* How could you possibly add psychiatric treatment into primary care without grinding the system to a halt?

---

157 Nodell, "Wayne Katon Obituary."

In a bit of serendipity, the outlines of a potential new approach had been developed by Dr. Katon's Seattle neighbor, Dr. Edward Wagner of Group Health Cooperative. Wagner was a primary care physician who experienced an awakening somewhat similar to Katon's. Whereas Dr. Katon saw psychiatric patients not receiving the treatment they needed, Dr. Wagner saw patients with chronic conditions not receiving the care *they* needed. As he looked closely at the existing state of care Wagner found a series of common deficiencies in the treatment of patients with chronic conditions including "rushed practitioners not following established practice guidelines, lack of care coordination, lack of active follow-up to ensure the best outcomes, [and] patients inadequately trained to manage their illness."[158]

Wagner worked to solve the problem by building what he called the *chronic care model*, designed to provide proactive care to patients with a variety of chronic conditions. Wagner and his team would not wait for these patients to show up in clinic with a litany of issues; they would keep a registry of patients and stay in contact with them to make sure they were getting the care they needed whether that was an office visit, new medications, dosage adjustments, whatever was needed.

The model, created by Wagner in the mid-1990s, was "designed to ... transform the daily care for patients with chronic illnesses from acute and reactive to proactive, planned, and population-based ... from a system that is essentially reactive—responding mainly when a person is sick—to one that is proactive and focused on keeping a person as healthy as possible." Ed Wagner was way ahead of his time. Proactive care, as we noted in earlier chapters, has become the gold standard in the US, and Wagner was one of the pioneers who recognized the power of those early interventions. *Health Affairs* magazine observed that "the evidence continues to pile up that the famed chronic-care

158 Improving Chronic Illness Care, "The Chronic Care Model."

model developed by Ed Wagner and colleagues at Group Health Puget Sound delivers superior patient care and health outcomes."[159]

D r. Katon thought it likely that the same principles that applied in managing chronic physical illness might work with mental conditions. The more Katon considered the idea, the more sense it made to him, and he set out to adapt the Wagner model to mental health. Several early efforts met with mixed results and fell short of the success Wagner had achieved with chronic conditions. But Katon and his mentee, Dr. Unützer, kept tinkering, and did so with a sense of urgency, aware that the mental health challenge in the US was enormous.

"As a psychiatrist, I'm here to tell you that mental health problems are not a rare thing," Unützer told a group at Vanderbilt University. "I have not met a family that hasn't been touched by a mental health or substance-abuse problem at some point in their lives." The challenge, he noted, was that:[160]

> In the next 12 months, only 1 out of 10 people in the US living with a diagnosable mental health or substance abuse problem will seek out a psychiatrist, while 2 out of 10 will see any kind of mental health specialist, and 4 out of 10 will see a primary care provider. But most will receive no formal treatment whatsoever. How would we feel about this if this was cancer? What if we said, of all the people living with cancer in the United States, in the next 12 months, 1 out of 10 will get to see a doctor who is trained to see patients with cancer? We would probably find that totally unacceptable.[161]

---

159 Ibid.
160 *NEJM Catalyst* event, "Expanding the Bounds of Care Delivery: Integrating Mental, Social, and Physical Health."
161 Ibid.

As they worked on the problem, Katon and Unützer hit upon a breakthrough idea. Instead of an individual psychiatrist caring for one patient at a time, it might work better if the psychiatrist served as a consultant to the primary care team. They introduced a *collaborative care model* which brought two new players into the primary care setting. The first is known as a behavioral health care manager while the second is a psychiatrist serving as a consultant (in other words, not meeting directly with patients but instead guiding the care manager and primary care physician on how best to treat patients). The care manager might be a nurse, psychologist, or a psychiatric social worker who takes responsibility for anywhere from fifty to one hundred and fifty patients. The care manager follows a series of pre-scribed steps: step one involves administering a standard screen for depression (which measures whether a patient is depressed and, if so, to what degree). The behavioral health manager then meets with the patient and discusses the case with a psychiatrist. Working together, the care manager and psychiatrist develop a treatment plan, updated weekly, for each patient. Thus, over time, all patients in the registry receive detailed attention. Run charts plot the progress of patients on their PHQ-9 scores and result in more intense focus on patients whose conditions are deteriorating. Some need new medications, higher dosages, or in some cases, a series of six to eight face-to-face problem-solving sessions with the care manager. At the other end of the spectrum are patients whose conditions improve over time and who graduate from the caseload.

The strength of the approach lies in its simplicity and use of the scarce resource that is a psychiatrist's time. This new way of deploying a psychiatrist is a game-changer, for it extends the psychiatrist's skill over a much larger population of patients than ever before. The mental health care manager is trained in a variety of brief, evidence-based interventions or counseling strategies for use in the primary care physician's office, and patients are tracked in a population-based registry tool to make sure they don't fall through the cracks. The team psychiatrist's role is to advise on what to do for patients who aren't showing signs of improvement and to occasionally see a patient in person or via telemedicine.

It is important to note that the Collaborative Care Model is one among a number of approaches that different provider organizations have taken to integrate behavioral health into primary care. Notable work is also being done at Southcentral Foundation in Anchorage and in the Cherokee Health System. "There are multiple approaches to integrating behavioral health and medical care," says Mara Laderman of the Institute for Healthcare Improvement, "and the type of approach an organization may select to implement will depend on their resources, population served, available providers, payment, etc."[162]

In theory, the Katon approach made sense, but to see whether it would work in practice, Dr. Unützer put it to the test in a trial on the frontlines of care. The study included 1,801 patients spread across eighteen primary care clinics in Washington, California, Texas, Indiana, and North Carolina. Stretching over a two-year period, the study focused on older adults suffering from depression. Half of the patients continued with whatever treatment constituted "usual care" within their clinic, while the other half were treated with the Collaborative Care Model.[163]

The results were definitive. The collaborative care approach

---

162 Laderman, interview with author.
163 AIMS Center, "Impact: Improving Mood – Promoting Access to Collaborative Treatment."

"more than doubled the effectiveness of depression treatment for older adults in primary care settings. At twelve months, about half of the patients receiving collaborative care reported at least a 50 percent reduction in depressive symptoms, compared with only 19 percent of those in usual care."[164]

Unützer noted that "more than 80 studies show us that if you do this right, you more than double the likelihood that somebody with a mental health or addiction problem will get well. There's also good research that shows that patients *like* this kind of care, doctors like this kind of care, and this is good business." For every $1 spent on collaborative care, health organizations gain back $7 in cost savings over the next four years.[165]

For every $1 spent on collaborative care, health organizations gain back $7 in cost savings over the next four years.

"That's the Triple Aim of health care reform right there," says Unützer. "That's better access, better quality, better outcomes for fewer health care dollars. That's dynamite."[166]

Among the first organizations to put it to the test was the Institute for Family Health, a federally qualified health center in New York City. In 2002 the organization received foundation funding to hire three behavioral health care managers to implement the program. Virna Little, the lead administrator, recalls that her organization already employed psychiatrists who served as consultants to the primary care team. With support and guidance from Jürgen Unützer and the University of Washington team, Little implemented the treatment approach. Primary care physicians knew they needed help and saw the

---

164 Ibid.
165 Aston, op. cit.
166 Ibid.

program as supporting their practice rather than adding new work. One of the roadblocks at the start was that the electronic health record had no template for results from depression-screening tests such as the PHQ-2. (If a patient is positive on the PHQ-2 screening tool then the more detailed PHQ-9 is administered.)

From the start, the system worked pretty much as designed by Unützer and associates. At each doctor visit the primary care physician would administer the PHQ-2 screen. When a patient was positive (about 10 percent of the early patients were, in fact, positive) the doctor would conduct a warm handoff to the care manager who would see the patient for a session that same day. This was a key element. Many patients, when referred for mental health treatment, skip the appointment out of anxiety or embarrassment.

"Treatment in a primary care office ... helps to ease a patient's concerns about the stigma still too often attached to mental illness. A doctor can just walk down a hall and introduce a patient to a counselor." When the patient meets the care manager in the comfort of the primary care doctor's office there is a greater degree of trust and comfort.[167]

Wayne Katon passed away in 2015, and an obituary from the University of Washington community described the influence of his work on medical science:

> Katon and colleagues showed that a collaborative intervention involving a psychiatrist working with primary care physicians significantly improved patients' adherence to medication, depressive outcomes, and satisfaction with care. More than 80 randomized controlled trials around the world have validated this approach since then ... In research published

---

167 AIMS Center, op. cit.

in 2010 in the *New England Journal of Medicine*, Katon and colleagues showed that collaborative care significantly improved not only the mental health but also the physical wellbeing of patients with poorly controlled heart disease and/or diabetes and comorbid depression.[168]

A subsequent study in 2016 covered a ten-year period and included 113,000 adults in primary care practices.

W e make no pretension that this work is easy. Adding behavioral health is a significant expansion to the primary care doctor's responsibility, which is why Wagner and others emphasize that the work is on the shoulders of the entire primary care team—case manager, medical assistant, nurse, and clinical pharmacist—not just the doctor. The shift demands that primary care physicians and their colleagues become comfortable with a whole new area of medicine, for which they did not train. Like so many other aspects that are changing in health care, this demands adaptability from everyone involved.

The trend to integrate behavioral health into primary care is so new that, as recently as 2013, Mara Laderman of the Institute for Healthcare Improvement says the question that most organizations asked was *why should we do it?* "Within the past several years the question has shifted from organizations wanting to know *why* they should do it to wanting to know *how* to do it," she told us. Rapidly growing numbers of organizations recognize that for the benefit of the overall health of the patient, integration of behavioral health in primary care is a necessity.[169]

As Laderman and Dr. Kedar Mate from IHI have written:

168 Nodell, op. cit.
169 Laderman, op.cit.

"Experts believe that behavioral health integration into primary care is on its way to becoming a new standard of care in the US."[170]

As keen as many organizations are to integrate behavioral health in primary care, Laderman says it doesn't happen easily: "There are a variety of clinical and operational barriers, and one of the main ones is cultural—how do you meld mental health and physical health cultures together?" Primary care physicians and mental health professionals are trained in very different ways, she notes:[171]

> Psychiatrists and many psychologists and other mental health providers trained to engage in deep, ongoing relationships with their patients through 50-minute sessions weekly or more frequently. But integrating behavioral health into primary care is very different—it's about brief interventions and problem solving. And primary care is not necessarily where a mental health provider wants to be.[172]

One of the significant challenges to integration is the management of patients' medications. Prior to the development of Prozac and related drugs in the late 1980s, it was unusual for a primary care physician to prescribe medications for patients with mental illness. This area of clinical pharmacology was highly specialized and done for the most part by trained psychiatrists. Prior to the existence of Prozac and other SSRI and SSNI classes of drugs, primary care physicians were generally reluctant to prescribe any of the powerful and potentially harmful medications psychiatrists previously used for patients with mental disorders. But Prozac and its cousins were medications with a significant upside and generally not much downside risk and

---

170 Laderman and Mate, "Integrating Behavioral Health into Primary Care."
171 Laderman, op. cit.
172 Ibid.

certainly not the dangerous downside risk of narcotics.

"Prozac changed everything," Diane Powers, from the department of psychiatry and behavioral sciences at the University of Washington, told us. "The side effects were much improved, and dosing was much more straightforward and simple. It was the kind of medicine where a primary care physician could say, 'okay, I could do that.'"[173]

Dr. Manish Sapra, our colleague at Northwell Health, explains:

> About 30 percent of what primary care physicians see in their practices involves psychiatry, and the reality is that the rest of stuff they deal with—chronic conditions and so forth—they are trained in, but they are not trained in psychiatry. And it used to be that prescribing anti-depressants was dangerous, because a depressed patient with two-weeks-worth of medication could use it to kill themselves. But with Zoloft, Prozac, and the other SSRIs it's really safe to use them. They have significantly fewer side effects and they are much safer—if you take a month's supply you will just get really sick to your stomach.[174]

Elements of the Collaborative Care Model

TEAM-DRIVEN ELEMENT

A multidisciplinary group of health care delivery professionals providing care in a coordinated fashion and who are empowered to work at the top of their professional training.

---

173 Powers, interview with author.
174 Sapra, interview with author.

POPULATION-FOCUSED ELEMENT

The collaborative care team is responsible for the provision of care and health outcomes of a defined population of patients.

MEASUREMENT-GUIDED ELEMENT

The team uses systematic, disease-specific, patient-reported outcome measures (e.g., symptom rating scales) to dive clinical decision-making.

EVIDENCE-BASED ELEMENT

The team adapts scientifically proven treatments within an individual clinical context to achieve improved health outcomes.

The major obstacle to spreading the collaborative care model is, as is so often the case in health care, financial. Who pays for adding a care manager and consulting psychiatrist to the primary care team? When Jürgen Unützer conducted the major trial he received foundation funding to support the work, as did Virna Little in New York. But the reality is that some provider organizations, already on thin financial ice, can ill afford the new hires. And yet, with the shift from fee-for-service payments to value-based care, there is now a growing incentive to make the investments in personnel:

> New payment models that reward providers for simultaneously improving health outcomes and reducing health care spending may provide an impetus for integrating behavioral health and primary care services. Such integration has long been recommended but has been difficult to achieve, because restrictive payment methods and practice patterns have impeded collaboration.[175]

---

175 Klein and Hostetter, "In Focus: Integrating Behavioral Health and Primary Care."

This changed on January 1, 2017, when CMS announced that, for Medicare patients, it would pay doctors separately for behavioral health services in primary care. (The change accelerated a year later when CMS approved three new billing codes that allowed for reimbursement of psychiatric-collaborative-care-management services.)[176]

The *New England Journal of Medicine* reported:

> Medicare's new payments for [behavioral health integration] will have their most immediate impact on clinicians already furnishing these services, who will now be paid more appropriately and accurately. But the biggest potential effect will be increasing the number of Medicare beneficiaries with access to effective [behavioral health integration] services. By one estimate, only about 10% of patients with depression (and less than 1% in some minority populations) receive guideline-concordant treatment under the status quo. Through systematic care management and more efficient use of behavioral health specialty providers, effective [behavioral health integration] produces more person-centered, coordinated, evidence-based care. It also helps build behavioral health competency in the primary care workforce. Studies have shown that [the Collaborative Care Model] improves the quality of care and patients' satisfaction with it, mental and physical health outcomes, and functioning in people with common behavioral health conditions, particularly— but not only—mood or anxiety disorders.[177]

Evidence also indicates that it can reduce total health care expenditures over time and can reduce racial and ethnic dis-

---

176 Press et al., "Medicare Payment for Behavioral Health Integration."
177 Ibid.

parities in quality of care and clinical outcomes. Therefore, widespread implementation of [the Collaborative Care Model] and other effective ... services could substantially improve outcomes for millions of Medicare beneficiaries, as well as produce savings for the Medicare program.

The best route toward payment—from commercial payers especially—ties back into what we explored in chapter two—paying for value rather than for volume. "Some health systems have been willing—at least in the short run—to absorb the costs of adding behavioral health services to primary care. For example, Boston Medical Center, an academic medical center and safety-net provider, is covering the cost of adding social workers, psychiatric nurse practitioners, and patient navigators into its family medicine practices on a trial basis. Part of the rationale is that the investment may help the medical center succeed in future value-based contracts."[178]

"According to a 2011 survey, 78 percent of primary care providers who have integrated behavioral health services into their practices said they pay for them with the help of grants."[179]

> There is ample evidence the Collaborative Care Model works, and it is time that commercial and government payers step up and provide the appropriate reimbursement for these essential services.

But why should providers have to rely upon foundation grants to provide highly valuable services to patients? And why should those highly valuable services not be something an insurance company, employer, or the government be willing to pay for? There is ample evidence the Collaborative Care

---

178 Klein and Hostetter, op. cit.
179 Ibid.

Model works, and it is time that commercial and government payers step up and provide the appropriate reimbursement for these essential services. As Dr. Marc Harrison, president and CEO of Intermountain Healthcare, put it: "Treating mental illness is expensive, but the cost of *not* treating it is enormous."[180]

B oston Medical Center is a safety-net organization, and the need for behavioral health capabilities is particularly important in such settings:

> Among people with a chronic condition, those with low incomes are much more likely (32%) to have a behavioral health condition than those with moderate incomes (24%) and those with high incomes (21%) ... Rates of serious psychological stress are much higher among low-income people with chronic and behavioral health problems (29%) compared to higher-income people with similar health conditions (7%).[181]

Within our own organization at Northwell Health, we have found, in the words of Dr. Joseph Conigliaro: "There is no clear-cut demarcation where behavioral health comorbidities start and where physical comorbidities end." Dr. Conigliaro, who serves as chief of general internal medicine for Northwell, says that "uncontrolled behavioral health issues make it difficult for people to comply with care guidelines for chronic conditions."[182]

We have found that someone with a chronic physical condition

---

180 Harrison, "It's Past Time to Include Mental Health Into the Doctor's Office Visit."

181 Cunningham, et al., "Income Disparities in the Prevalence, Severity, and Costs of Co-Occurring Chronic and Behavioral Health Conditions."

182 Kenney, op. cit.

as well as depression may very well lack the energy to do the kinds of things that improve his or her health. Many people in these circumstances simply become overwhelmed by the combination of physical and mental illnesses. Within our practices we integrate behavioral health with primary care and screen for depression, anxiety, and other emotional issues just as we screen for diabetes or cancer. Such screenings are so essential that we think of the PHQ2 screening tool as constituting an additional vital sign. Our physicians screen not only for behavioral health concerns but for lifestyle issues that adversely affect health, such as tobacco, drug, or alcohol use:

"When a patient with diabetes or congestive heart failure or any number of issues also has depression, anxiety, or schizophrenia, providing consistent care becomes much more challenging," says Conigliaro. The federal government has created incentives, administered by the states, to help doctors redesign their practices to integrate behavioral health capabilities into primary care more effectively. This program has helped Conigliaro and his colleagues establish teams of health coaches available to patients by telephone. The coaches help guide patients by answering their questions and steering them to the appropriate type of care, depending upon their condition."[183]

"Oftentimes patients don't need care from the Emergency Room, but they don't know that," says Conigliaro. "Health coaches help them understand the best options."[184]

In some instances, coaches connect the patient with pharmacists for a medication adjustment, while in others the coach sets up an office appointment for the patient with a doctor or nurse. We are fortunate to be located primarily in the state of New York where the Delivery System Reform Incentive Payment program (DSRIP)

---

183 Ibid.
184 Ibid.

"brings internists to inpatient psychiatric units to address medical needs on site." This is obviously different than embedding a behavioral health professional in primary care, yet it accomplishes the same thing—that is, making sure patients get their physical and mental health care in the same place where they know and trust the team.[185]

"For some people, it's all we can do to connect them to psychiatric care, so this setup addresses both types of health concerns without disrupting the system," Dr. Conigliaro said, adding that it further engages patients in their own care. At Northwell we have embedded a psychologist, social worker, or mental health counselor within primary care clinics and given these team members access to an off-site consulting psychiatrist.[186]

I n 1999, when Surgeon General David Satcher convened a national meeting on mental health and issued a landmark report, the idea of integrating behavioral health capabilities into primary care seemed far-fetched. But the innovations in primary care led by Dr. Wagner and continued and enhanced by Drs. Katon and Unützer, led to a fundamental change in the way care is delivered to patients with mental health issues. The change in attitude—that behavioral health should be an integral part of primary care—is an historic shift in thinking that is benefitting more and more people. In America, we are nowhere near caring for all of the patients who need behavioral health treatment, but with this new pathway in primary care, we are making progress.

---

185 Ibid.
186 Kenney, op. cit.

CHAPTER SEVEN

Consumerism: Measures that Actually Matter to Patients!

"We've never really measured [what mattered to patients] very well because nobody really cared about it."

Back around 2008, more than a few prognosticators predicted a consumer revolution in health care. Transparency in pricing and quality measures would prompt American consumers to purchase health care in the same way they purchased every other product or service: actively comparing price, quality, convenience, etc.

Consumers had used the internet to disrupt every other industry, including banking, travel, and retail. Health care was up next. And, in a way, there *has* been something of a revolution: Internet sites such as Google and WebMD provide patients with much more detailed information about an array of medical conditions than was ever before widely available. Many patients use the sites to deepen knowledge about illnesses they or family members face. Others cherry-pick online information and grow fearful they might be suffering from some dreaded malady. Patients showed up clutching Google printouts with detailed questions and no small amount of anxiety. Some doctors were chagrined by this shift in the doctor-patient power gradient, others embraced it.

There seems little doubt that having better informed patients is a step in the right direction, but there *is* doubt about whether patients are behaving as savvy health care consumers. In fact, there is plenty of evidence that they are not doing so and that the long-awaited consumer revolution may be some ways off. At the end of 2015, for example, a McKinsey consulting team reported that five surveys they conducted suggest that:

> Many, if not most, health care consumers are not yet making research-based decisions. Our findings indicate ... that only a few consumers are currently researching provider costs or even the number of providers they can choose among. Although some (but far from most) consumers are beginning to research their health plan choices, many of them are not yet aware of key factors they should consider before selecting coverage.[187]

Many people believed that transparency of prices and quality ratings could change the dynamic, but the evidence for this is slim, and in fact, a 2016 report found that "offering a price transparency tool was not associated with lower health care spending and that only a small percentage of eligible employees at the two large companies studied used the tool."[188]

A 2016 survey of adults enrolled in high-deductible health plans found that "only 14 percent compared prices and quality ratings."

---

187 Cordina, et al., "Debunking Common Myths About Healthcare Consumerism."

188 Dafny and Mohta, "New Marketplace Survey: What's Next for Payment Reform?"

Fourteen percent!? Imagine the percentage of Americans who would shop around on price and quality for a new car or computer. Why, then, only 14 percent in health care?[189]

Martin Gaynor, a health economist at Carnegie Mellon University, suggested that the 20 percent of patients who account for 80 percent of health care spending are facing serious medical issues that are covered by insurance and therefore have little incentive to comparison shop. Such patients, says Gaynor, "have expenses that put them beyond the cost-sharing features of any (reasonable) health insurance plan"—a very good thing for the patient. But Gaynor says that it "means that they have no reason to pay attention to costs" and that "the overwhelming majority of health expenses are incurred by people who are not going to shop on the basis of cost and therefore won't force providers to compete on costs." Furthermore, he says, "consumers have a lot of inertia and are often poorly informed. This should make us cautious about how well consumers will make decisions."[190]

Harvard health economist Amitabh Chandra studied the behavior of consumers enrolled in high-deductible plans and found "no evidence of consumers learning to price shop after two years in high-deductible coverage." Why was this? There are a number of reasons, but surely one of the key elements, as Chandra observes, is that "in health care, the consumer (i.e., the patient) is sick, tired, confused, distracted."[191]

Fortunately, there is an aspect of the consumer movement in health care that has made important progress and promises to alter, perhaps significantly, the way doctors and other providers think about how best

---

189 Haefner, "Survey: Most Americans with High-Deductible Health Plans Don't Shop for Care: 5 Things to Know."
190 Ibid.
191 Ibid.

to measure quality. When Dr. Ira Kirschenbaum, an experienced orthopedic surgeon, was asked to name landmark moments in orthopedics during recent decades, he offered a surprising point of view. Important strides have been made in both surgical techniques and the quality of the devices used to replace human knees, hips, and more, but Dr. Kirschenbaum identified a very different sort of progress.

"Probably the greatest advance in orthopedics in the past two decades has been the way we look at the success or failure of treatment interventions," he said:[192]

> There has been a shift in focus on what the surgeon views as a success versus what the patient views a success. In 1995, we thought we knew that when a patient reached certain postsurgical parameters, it was called a success. *We have since realized that the patient's view of satisfaction is more important* [emphasis added]. In 2015, we talk about 'patient-reported outcomes' rather than specific surgical scoring systems. That has been a radical shift.[193]

This shift from defining quality from the physician's perspective to defining quality from a patient perspective is historic—and it is one of the most important trends in health care today. The new focus asks simple questions: Can the woman with a new knee walk and play with her grandchildren? Can the man in his sixties who has had prostate

This shift from defining quality from the physician's perspective to defining quality from a patient perspective is historic—and it is one of the most important trends in healthcare today.

192 Kirschenbaum, "Landmarks in Orthopedics: A Twenty-Year Perspective."
193 Ibid.

surgery avoid incontinence?

"We have also seen a shift in the focus from looking only at long-term clinical results of surgery to looking at more immediate results," Kirschenbaum continues. "In 2015, we care much more about enhanced, pain-free surgery and rapid recovery. Whether this is an emotional patient satisfaction issue or a practical issue of earlier return to function is unclear, but no doubt it dominates the discussion in a way that it didn't back in 1995."[194]

Kirschenbaum makes another cogent point when he echoes the cry of many health care professionals that doctors and hospitals are suffering from metric fatigue, forced by the government, insurers, and regulatory agencies, to report hundreds of measures to the point where what is measured today is often less than fully meaningful even as it drains time and energy from physicians and administrators.

How out-of-control is metric overload? Medicare estimates that doctors in the US spend an average of "more than 785 hours per year to report quality measures under the current system"—an average of fifteen hours per week! The industry needs to reach a consensus on a manageable number of quality metrics that are excellent representatives of whether patients are receiving quality care. Kirschenbaum calls for action to "streamline quality measures and focus on what patients care about most: functional status, a good experience, fewer complications, and better outcomes."[195]

---

194 Ibid.

195 Casalino et al., "US Physician Practices Spend More Than $15.4 Billion Annually to Report Quality Measures"; Kirschenbaum, op. cit.

850
Centers for Medicare and Medicaid Services (CMS) Measures

635
National Quality Forum (NQF) Endorsed Measures
Medicaid Delivery System Reform Incentive Payment (DSRIP), NYS Patient Occurrence Reporting And Tracking System (NYPORTS), NYSDOH Stroke, NYSDOH Sepsis, NYSDOH HAI, Communicable Disease, NYSDOH Cardiac

546
Private Health Plan Measures
Registries, Voluntary Collaboratives, The Joint Commission, ANCC Magnet Status, Patient-centered Medical Home, Accountable Care Organizations (ACOS), NDNQI Nurse Sensitive Measures

100+
Delivery System Reform Incentive Payment (DSRIP) Measures
Consumer Report Cards, Managed Care Plans

33
Accountable Care Organization Measures
Value-based Purchasing, Meaningful Use, Patient Safety, CMS Sepsis Medicare Readmissions, Medicare Inpatient Quality, Medicare Outpatient Quality, Patient Experience, Mortality, Hospital-acquired Conditions (HACS), Physician Quality

A study of several dozen oncologists and their patients revealed a gulf between what mattered most to patients versus what mattered most to doctors:

> To a physician, doing the job well may mean following practice guidelines carefully. To a patient, it could mean something quite different—whether the physician listens well or provides important test results promptly.[196]

Indeed, the study found that doctors and patients agreed on the importance of certain elements such as technical proficiency and coordination of care. But the study also found that "patients highlighted some things doctors missed such as having enough time with their doctor, access to social services, help dealing with the bureaucracy, and convenient treatment.[197]

Listening to patients, we learn that attitudes are shifting with the generations. Younger people, for example, live on their smartphones and want all of their health care information there as well. And they want it *now*.

Health care metrics have evolved over time. In the 1990s or early 2000s, most focused on process. These were and remain important because "good outcomes are dependent on the building blocks of process," in the words of our colleague Dr. Mark Jarrett, chief quality officer at Northwell. Process metrics measure whether certain standard processes were followed: Did a heart-attack patient receive cholesterol medicine before leaving the hospital? Did a patient receive an antibiotic prior to surgery? Was the central line inserted

---

196 Greene, "When Value Is in the Eye of the Patient."
197 Ibid.

according to precise safety rules?[198]

Scott Wallace at Dartmouth has noted that "of the 123 different metrics in the government's *Hospital Compare* website, 102 measure processes. That's important, but it has become too burdensome for the benefit it delivers."[199]

RATINGS GAME

Government and industry organizations use hundreds of different metrics to evaluate the quality of health care delivered in the US. The measures fall into four broad categories:

Process:
What is being measured: how care matches recommended protocols
Example: Are diabetes patients given foot and eye exams?

Outcomes:
What is being measured: how patients fare as a result of care
Example: How many patients survive surgery?

Experience:
What is being measured: how patients evaluate the care received
Example: Did the doctor explain options understandably?

Structure:
What is being measured: how well-equipped care setting is to deliver care
Example: Does the office have an electronic prescribing system?

As Dr. Kirschenbaum has observed, the emphasis has shifted to measuring outcomes including mortality, rates of readmission to the

198 Jarrett, interview with author.
199 Beck, "What Measures Should Be Used to Evaluate Healthcare?"

hospital, hospital-acquired infections, and the like. In recent years, the measurement focus has begun to shift toward measuring what matters most to patients. The assumption underlying this approach is that when a patient is operated on for a new hip, for example, the basics will be done expertly. Dr. Jarrett says the expectation in such cases is that in a highly reliable organization "you try to approach perfection"—no infections, no dislocation of the prothesis, no unmanaged pain in rehab, etc. "But if you are the patient you want to know 'how soon can I go back to work afterwards? How soon can I drive a car? How soon can I go play golf or go to the mall and shop?' To the patient, those are the things about their quality of life.'"[200]

Importantly, the federal government is pushing in this direction with what it calls a "meaningful measures" program. The Centers for Medicare & Medicaid Services has reduced from about one hundred in 2017 to thirty-two in 2018 the number of measures it requires of provider organizations involved with Medicare quality programs as well as value-based purchasing contracts. The measurement movement "is moving in the direction of outcomes-based measurement," IHI's Dr. Kedar Mate told the publication *Modern Healthcare,* adding that "what we want to do is measure the things that matter the most, and the only judge and jury of that are the patients we serve."[201]

Virtually every major provider organization is pursuing this approach in some fashion. Dr. Amy Compton-Phillips, chief clinical officer at Providence-St. Joseph Health, talks about measures for hip and knee replacement surgery:

> There are a lot of measures that you can look at on whether or not you're doing well with hips and knees, and it's everything

---

200 Jarrett, op. cit.
201 Castelucci, "Will CMS' Efforts to Limit Quality Reporting to 'Meaningful Measures' pay off? Stakeholders Aren't Sure."

from length of stay, to infection rates, to revision rates, to all these inside baseball measures. And if you ask [patients] why they get their hip replaced, they would very rarely tell you [it's] to avoid a hospital readmission or to shorten the length of stay ... They want their function to be better.[202]

Dr. Compton-Phillips wanted a set of metrics that would represent the idea of providers "giving a darn." She looked at various measure sets from different organizations including Medicare, the American Orthopaedic Association, and others, and she created "a superset to start narrowing down what the measures of the *give-a-darn* test would be. The ones that passed the test were things like functional status ... infection rates ... length of stay. It was really things that made a difference to patients' outcomes that made it onto our short list."[203]

Dr. Jarret believes one way to advance the cause of patient-centered measures is to personalize stories:

I try [to] get people presenting a case not to say 'a 75-year-old male, who has history of high blood pressure and diabetes presents with a swollen leg.' Instead, let's say 'a 75-year-old man, who has diabetes and is a grandfather of three, likes to play golf, and is a retired sergeant from the NYPD.' When you humanize it, it brings everybody back to the patient. Ten or fifteen years ago a lot of people would have said that's a little too touchy-feely, but now people understand it and it's good to humanize health care. Medicine is changing.[204]

---

202 Compton-Phillips, "The 'Give a Darn' Method for Outcomes Measurement."
203 Ibid.
204 Jarrett, op. cit.

F or many years, and to a large extent even today, the most significant measure in medicine was the reputation of a medical center, physician group, or individual doctor. Critical questions included: What is a hospital's rank on the *US News* list? Which physicians make a local magazine's *doctors-doctors-go-to* list? As we've seen, the array of metrics in health care is staggering. Doctors and hospitals are measured by governments at the state and federal level, by insurance companies, by some employers, by consumer and advocacy groups, and by themselves. The great majority of provider organizations maintain an ongoing dashboard, measuring the metrics they consider the most important, whether for patient satisfaction, safety, reimbursements, etc.

Into the metric madness comes Michael Porter, the Harvard Business School professor, whose book, *Redefining Healthcare* (written with Elizabeth Teisburg), is a classic. Porter, who has been working on health care for many years, possesses a keen understanding of measurement and he has come up with new and potentially dynamic ways of measuring what really matters in health care. In 2012, Porter collaborated with Stefan Larsson at the Boston Consulting Group and Martin Ingvar at the Karolinska Institute in Stockholm to establish universal measures of quality that could be used by providers, payers, and patients throughout the world. To further this ambitious undertaking the three men formed the International Consortium for Health Outcomes Measurement (ICHOM). The organization "grew out of the conviction that the universal development and reporting of patient outcomes by medical condition is the single greatest enabler of delivery system transformation."[205]

ICHOM "works with patients, leading providers, and registries to create a global standard for measuring results by medical

---

205 Harvard Business School Institute for Strategy and Competitiveness, "International Consortium for Health Outcomes Measurement."

condition, from prostate cancer to coronary artery disease." The goal is to define measures focused on how well the care lives up to patient expectations:[206]

> Doctors think about prostate cancer in terms of PSA levels. The average patient doesn't. That's why we need to change how we evaluate and talk to patients about their health. At ICHOM, [they're] developing a new paradigm focused on health outcomes—the results that matter most to patients. The end result? A world where patients ask their doctors about meaningful outcomes, and doctors can respond with data-driven answers. To [ICHOM], it's more than improving the doctor-patient relationship. [They're] creating a new definition of success that transforms health care in several important ways.[207]

Ultimately, ICHOM aspires "to ensure that value-based health care becomes a reality, and this can happen only if all the system participants are committed to health outcomes ... that represent true success in managing the specified medical condition." Quality is about "focus on how well the care delivered meets individual patients' needs" and not just in the aftermath of surgery or hospitalization.[208]

"Measuring success, or the results of treatment, requires following the patient through the process of care and looking at medical conditions and patients holistically. For example, for patients with diabetes, their medical condition includes co-existing hypertension, renal disease, and retinal disease. Success in treating diabetes incorporates the combined effect of caring for all of these needs." This is perhaps

---

206 Ibid.
207 Ibid.
208 Ibid.

the most ambitious and, arguably, most patient-centered method of measurement out there.[209]

ICHOM has set up dozens of expert working groups focused on specific diseases. The working group on coronary artery disease, for example:

> Identified a consensus standard set of outcomes for the spectrum of patients with a diagnosis of [the disease] in order to provide a foundation for making appropriate comparisons among countries and health systems in efforts to improve quality. The set incorporates frequently unreported outcomes that are important to patients, such as symptom burden and quality of life, as well as traditional outcomes such as mortality ... The Working Group recommended not only short-term in-hospital outcomes but longer-term (1- and 5-year) outcomes.[210]

And because these patient-reported outcomes require significant effort on the part of physicians and their teams, ICHOM recommends focusing on only a few, well-selected metrics which emphasize "symptom burden, functional status, and health-related quality of life."[211]

Porter is an ardent believer in payment reform and he and his colleagues suggest that as "public and private payers alike are transitioning toward value-based reimbursement [the] ICHOM Standard Sets allow [them] not only to measure the immediate outcomes achieved but also the appropriateness of care and the long-term effects on what really matters to patients."[212]

---

209 Ibid.
210 Ibid.
211 Ibid.
212 ICHOM, "Why Measure Outcomes?"

For a very long time in health care, we have been so provider-focused that the relatively new emphasis on the patient really is a welcome development. Like every other major provider organization in the country, we here at Northwell focus intensively on the patient experience. While we do many of the things others do, we have also taken a somewhat different tack. For starters, we brought in as chief experience officer a man with extensive experience in the hospitality industry. Sven Gierlinger formerly worked in major roles at Ritz-Carlton Hotels and at Henry Ford Health System. He told us:

> What we think of as patient experience has evolved over time. It started with patient advocacy, then it turned into what was called service excellence, which was mostly—when you really peeled the onion—a complaint department. And then it turned a little bit more proactive, and now we're talking about the patient experience where we are actually integrating that into the quality of care.[213]

Focusing on patient-centered outcomes means asking, over and over again, *what matters to you?*

Focusing on patient-centered outcomes means asking, over and over again, *what matters to you?* And when you ask that question, you better be prepared to act on what you hear back from patients.

"Consistency is most important," says Gierlinger. "Delivering high-touch, empathetic care each and every time is what patients desire and deserve. Failure to deliver such care is where breakdowns begin and, our research shows, that is what they remember."[214]

---

213 Gierlinger, interview with author.
214 Ibid.

How does an organization put that kind of information to use? We sat down with various teams and said, okay, what is the obvious conclusion here? And the obvious conclusion based on feedback from our patients was that in our business of taking care of people, we have to make every moment count because *every encounter with a patient matters to that patient.* In other words, in some industries you might be doing well getting the customer experience right 90-plus percent of the time, but in our business, we don't have that kind of margin. We have to get it right every time or our patients will not have the kind of experience they want and deserve. Like so much else in health care, this becomes a cultural issue. How do you embed within the culture the idea that every interaction is a moment of truth? That every interaction, no matter how small it might seem to a staff person, matters to a patient?

And the answer is that there is no easy answer—except to listen to what patients tell you and change and improve based on that feedback. Gierlinger says we might have patients who came in through the emergency department with significant conditions of some kind. And over several days our doctors and nurses and technicians do an outstanding job, perhaps even saving the patient's life, stabilizing them, and sending them home in good shape. And then, on a survey, the patients recall that when they were in the ED, they experienced a good deal of pain when the IV was inserted.

"Now, we can react to that in one of two ways," says Gierlinger:

We can say, 'well, sorry about that but we did provide timely and quality care after all.' Or we can reflect and say, 'you know, we need to do a better job of explaining, educating, and inserting IVs so we cause minimal discomfort to patients, so let's put in place some training to accomplish that.' This is one example of specific feedback we have received when interviewing patients about their experience in our hospitals. Our goal is consistency of quality and empathic care, and it's our responsibility to listen to the voice of our patients in order to effectuate change.[215]

How does someone with experience at the Ritz-Carlton fit into this work?

"I get that question a lot," Gierlinger tells us:

People often say to me, 'how do you compare the hotel industry with the health care industry?' And I think, at a fundamental level, both of them are in the relationship business, and the relationship drives success or failure within that. If you look at health care, it's the ultimate relationship business, because we have the most intimate relationships with patients. We know more about them than their friends and family do, if you think about it. So trust really drives that relationship. At Ritz-Carlton, we had the Ritz-Carlton credo, and actually, I've taken the credo, and thought about that in the context of health care, and it translates really well. It talks about 'the genuine care and comfort of our guests is our highest mission. We pledge to provide the finest personal service and facilities for our guest[s], who will always enjoy a warm, relaxed, yet refined ambiance. The Ritz-Carlton experience enlivens the senses, instills wellbeing, and fulfills the expressed and unexpressed wishes of our guests.' If you just take 'Ritz-Carlton' out and put 'health care' in, and you change 'guests' to 'patients,' that resonates, because genuine care and comfort are what patients are looking for. It's even more important to provide that genuine care to someone

215 Ibid.

who's vulnerable, who's sick, than somebody who's checking in for pleasure or for business or whatever it is. And if you can take the excellence in medical care and everything that comes with it, and you take the service piece and you wrap it around that, then you have a perfect product.[216]

And that health care "product" actually gets higher marks from patients who are in value-based payment contracts, a further indication of the alignment between payment reform and quality. In value-based contracts, proactive, upstream care is required to manage a patient's comorbidities to prevent readmissions, etc.

"Those kinds of steps have an impact on patient satisfaction," Gierlinger says, "because if you manage and navigate the medical conditions, you help them manage the entire encounter in their medical life, so to speak. If we look at the satisfaction of our patients that are in some of those risk arrangements, it's tremendous how that actually jumps up."[217]

While patient experience and outcomes are measured, so too are doctors. It was not so very many years ago that physicians were rarely graded on anything after medical school or training.

In retrospect, that seems odd. Among the brightest people in society, doctors are traditionally more than comfortable being tested and graded from childhood through their late twenties or early thirties when the grading ends abruptly. No longer. In health care now, the grading for physicians never ends. Dr. Ira Nash, senior vice president at Northwell, makes an important point suggesting that "the reason why we traditionally went from 'hyper-grading' in college and med school to 'no grading' in clinical training and practice is that until

216 Ibid.
217 Ibid.

relatively recently, no one believed that one could measure clinical quality in a meaningful way. The real revolution is that quality is now looked at as something measurable."[218]

Reasonable people can argue the merits of this approach, but the reality is that in a consumer-centric world where just about every product and service is rated by consumers online, the same is happening in health care. While many physicians are justifiably concerned with posting individual ratings—these things are inherently complex—there is also a growing recognition among physicians that in the new, data-rich world, disclosure of physician ratings is inevitable.

"The ground has been prepared for this effort by the fact that people see all around them that everything is getting rated," Nash told us. "I said from the beginning that 'this isn't about whether you want to be rated or not, this is about whether you want Yelp to do it or Health Grades to do it or Vitals or Web MD or whatever' … We now publish on our own website the patient experience scores and comments that patients provide through Press Ganey."[219]

Dr. Nash started by providing individual physicians with measures of their own performance. "We created a scorecard that every doc got emailed to him or her directly," he said. "'Here are your scores. Here's how to compare it to everybody in your department. Here's how you compare to a national sample of people who practice in your discipline and here's how you're tracking over time.'"[220]

Initially, these scores were seen only by the individual physician and his or her clinical leader. After a period of time, Nash upped the ante and results of individual physician scores were published on an intranet site accessible to any clinician within a given practice. This

---

218 Kenney, op. cit.
219 Ibid.
220 Ibid.

was eye-opening. Now every doctor could see how they compared on important measures to colleagues in similar practices.

Dr. Mark Jarrett, chief quality officer at Northwell, has pushed for more real-time data as a way for doctors to learn and improve. "Getting performance data in real time is important to performance improvement," he says. "Real-time data gets people to think, 'these are not just numbers—this is somebody's grandmother or somebody's mother or somebody's sister or brother or child.' That is important if you are going to develop a really and truly highly reliable organization. Because people have to think about everything they are doing and are they doing it the right way and not cutting corners."[221]

In real-time measurement, Jarrett focuses on lowest preventable mortality with an emphasis on best practices to head off hospital-acquired conditions such as central-line infections, surgical-site infections, pressure ulcers, falls with injuries, sepsis, etc. While Dr. Jarrett studies data for the entire Northwell system, he also drills down to the unit level:

> So that every nursing unit will know how they are doing. It is important because it is really the front-line troops who really make the change. Leaders can get people motivated, but true performance improvement comes from front-line people saying, 'this is the way it works. This is what we have got to do.' We have a lot of system-level stuff and hospital-level stuff and now we are bringing it down to the unit level.[222]

Jarrett says that sharing comparative data with various hospitals and clinics can spur improvement. Every month at a meeting of medical directors from the twenty-three Northwell hospitals, Jarrett

---

221 Jarrett, op. cit.
222 Ibid.

displays a slide with the latest infection rates for each facility.

"Having that data out there pulls everybody up a little bit, because they do not want to be the one [who] had four of these infections last month when everybody else had only one last month. It motivates them to push a little harder."[223] Typically, quality relates to clinical outcomes, but in an age when the cost of care is so steep Jarrett believes that it is necessary to include the concept of value within the quality equation. Value, in one sense, means eliminating unneeded care—"when we do things we do not need to do [that] increase risk for the patient" and drive up costs. Changing the way doctors do certain things is not easy. *You mean to tell me I have been doing it wrong all these years!?*[224]

"There is the difficulty of abandoning things that you learned a long time ago that seemed to work, but now the data says that you should change and abandon what you are doing," observes Dr. Lawrence Smith:[225]

> Do it a different way, because the outcomes are better. That is a psychic struggle that many physicians have difficulty with. What you were doing was not wrong. It is just that now there is evidence that there is a better way to do it. I think that getting people to understand that collecting data about their own outcomes is not about gotcha. It is about continuous improvement. The data is not a personal assault for which you should have an emotional reaction. It is simply information to allow you to continuously get better. As care delivery evolves new research indicates that, for example, there is no clinical evidence to support testing

223 Ibid.
224 Ibid.
225 Kenney, op. cit.

for prostate cancer in low-risk patients over age 70. To get physicians to change is only possible through the use of good data; data indicating that perhaps there may be a better way than the way they [have] been trained and doing something for years or even decades.[226]

Says Jarrett: "It's really about education and showing them the data."[227]

Could the consumer movement accelerate? It is possible, though by no means certain, that the pace of change will quicken. Is there a tipping point out on the horizon where market forces in health care and the inherently savvy consumer nature of Americans merges? There are experts at McKinsey who think so. In an analysis of marketplace changes—high-deductible health-insurance plans, narrow provider networks, increasing copays, etc.—the McKinsey folks see change ahead. They write:

> Until recently, consumerism in the US health care industry has moved slowly. However, several converging forces are likely to change the situation soon and result in a more dynamic market. Higher deductibles and copayments, greater transparency into provider performance and costs, and the rise of network-narrowing and provider-led health plans are prodding patients to become more involved in health care decision-making than ever before ... We believe that health care consumerism will soon ... become a much more significant force.[228]

---

226 Ibid.
227 Jarrett, op. cit.
228 Shaywitz, op. cit.

There are certain aspects of care where we think this kind of consumerism is likely. For example, when a patient needs an imaging test and the cost for one at an independent location is about half what it costs at a tertiary hospital, that patient may well go for the lower cost. But for most patients—especially the sickest patients who account for most health care costs? We tend to think that Amitabh Chandra is right as we noted above—that "in health care, the consumer (i.e., the patient) is sick, tired, confused, distracted."

This is one of the newest and most important major trends in health care in the United States, and it will require time before it fully takes root.

"We're still an immature field in terms of determining patient-centered outcomes," says Jarrett. "We've never really measured it very well because nobody really cared about it. We focused on infections, readmissions, etc." Nonetheless, the shift within the industry to the things that truly matter to patients is one of the most welcome trends in health care in the twenty-first century.[229]

229 Jarrett, op. cit.

CHAPTER EIGHT

Consolidation: Merger Mania

"The problem is not consolidation, per se,
but consolidation without integration."

I n American lore there are few images as winning as the small-town doctor, black bag in hand, on a two o'clock in the morning house call to a distressed neighbor. There is something iconic in the combination of specialized knowledge and tireless commitment to patients at any hour, day or night. This physician not only eased suffering but also served as a pillar of the community—a person whose judgement was sought on a wide variety of issues beyond medicine, an independent thinker who hung up a shingle and served people free of any encumbrances. Recalling those days evokes an image of an earlier, simpler time that, in retrospect, feels authentically American and deeply appealing.

But the reality in the twenty-first century, as harsh as it may feel in the distant glow of that earlier time, is that those days are gone; that the idea of a standalone physician practice in the current marketplace, with rare exceptions, is part of the past. And the standalone hospital is not far behind. The reality of the current economic climate makes going it alone, for a physician or hospital, no longer viable. It is too often the case that smaller provider entities lack the critical mass needed to adapt to the rapid expansion of medical knowledge and to deliver care that integrates the latest breakthroughs.

Consolidation is one of the most powerful forces in health care and, in the years ahead, all signs indicate that it will only accelerate. Many analysts have compared health care to other industries that have experienced significant consolidation, including airlines, banking, and retail. All three have been profoundly disrupted in recent years to the point where there are "95 percent fewer US department store chains … in operation today than in the 1960s;" half as many banks as in 1990; and 75 percent fewer US passenger airlines than in the 1970s.[230]

Could health care experience a similarly radical consolidation? It certainly seems as though the industry is in the midst of such a change. There is an air of inevitability to the consolidation trend, which is leading the nation to a point where there will soon be very few small health care organizations left. The technology, analytics, and the ability to manage populations of patients while engaging with the social determinants of health, etc., require size as well as clinical and financial strength. Dr. Thomas Schwenk puts it this way: "It is becoming increasingly clear that the political and economic forces driving changes in the delivery and reimbursement of medical care will eventually lead to new practice models that are likely to be … unsustainable by small, private, stand-alone medical practices."[231]

Every major industry in the United States is fiercely competitive, and health care is no exception. The reality of the modern marketplace is that organizations must continually grow both organically and via

---

230 Skillrud, et al., "The Great Consolidation: The Potential for Rapid Consolidation of Health Systems."

231 Schwenk, "Integrated Behavior and Primary Care."

mergers in order to survive. Insurers, suppliers, and pharma continue to grow and consolidate, and they prey upon provider organizations that remain static. It is clear from our own experiences and those of other major organizations throughout the country that the benefits to consolidation and integration are numerous. It facili-

The reality of the modern marketplace is that organizations must continually grow both organically and via mergers in order to survive.

tates more experimentation and innovation and allows for expansion of services and increased back-office efficiency.

Significantly, consolidation and integration improve access to capital needed to acquire, improve, or partner with smaller hospitals that are in financial trouble. A Deloitte analysis found that financial pressures, technological innovations, as well as regulatory changes are driving significant vertical (a hospital purchasing a physician practice) and horizontal (a hospital purchasing or merging with another hospital) consolidation. Drawing from the lessons of retail, banking, and airlines, Deloitte found that "market drivers prompted industry participants to buy, sell, or merge with other entities to gain scale or enhanced capabilities that could enable them to more effectively compete."[232]

The Deloitte analysis projected that this period in health care consolidation will cut the number of health systems in the United States *in half*. By any measure, such a change would represent a radical realignment of the landscape. The conclusion seems inescapable that thousands of health systems existing today will be acquired or merged into other entities in the coming years, while some will go out of

---

232 Skillrud, et al., "The Great Consolidation: The Potential for Rapid Consolidation of Health Systems."

business completely. Instinctively, this is viewed as a lamentable development, and certainly, in cases where jobs and access to care are lost, it is deeply lamentable. The Deloitte consultants argue that there are a variety of different pathways forward for provider organizations, but that the status quo is not a viable choice. They write:

> Staying the course is no longer an option; organizations should prepare by either differentiating to maintain dominance in a clinical or geographic niche or acquiring or aligning with other health systems. Those that do not act promptly and strategically may face major risks, including loss of significant market share or loss of local control as a result of being acquired.[233]

There seems little doubt that new payment models, particularly the shift from fee-for-service to value-based payments, are accelerating the consolidation trend. Payment reform "requires health systems to make bold strategic decisions: differentiate through innovation, diversify, or manage a population's health risk. Few health systems have the financial and organizational wherewithal to 'go it alone' and accomplish these strategies."[234]

A report from the consultancy Charles River Associates found that "new payment initiatives that require providers to become financially responsible for the outcomes of the services they provide and the general health status of the population they treat also demand scale in order to mitigate the risk of high-cost patients. Without sufficient patient volumes, a few unusually high-cost patients can undermine an otherwise stable financial position."[235]

233 Ibid.
234 Ibid.
235 Noether and May, "Hospital Merger Benefits: Views from Hospital Leaders and Econometric Analysis."

Dan Mendelson, the president of Avalere, a health care consulting company, told the *Washington Post*:

Health care is increasingly about the ability of medical enterprises to deliver improved patient care through technology. All insurers are interested in developing a strong presence in data analytics. This in turn encourages mergers and acquisitions. Why? CVS is a diversified health care company with operations in pharmacy benefit management, post-acute care, and a strong network of health care clinics—it's not just a drug store chain. By merging with CVS, Aetna gains access to these rich data sources to drive better health care practices. The same is true for CVS in reverse. It gets to tap Aetna's databases and discover, say, which of its policyholders haven't received their flu shot and could be solicited by CVS ... The pace of big combinations will accelerate in coming years. All health care companies will need to reposition themselves to accommodate the fundamental trends of the health care system—which will continue irrespective of political change ... payers—private insurers and government through Medicare and Medicaid—are paying more for value (good patient outcomes) as opposed to the volume of services (the number of tests and procedures). Medicare and Medicaid have led the way, but private insurers are catching up. This has driven consolidation in the provider sectors (hospitals and doctors), because it's easier to measure and improve quality as a system as opposed to influencing sole-proprietor or small-group practices. This has also driven the acquisition of providers by insurers, because the key to improving quality is getting a better alignment between the interests of patients and providers. A second major trend is related: the increasing role of information technology and data analytics in improving patient care. A lot of the basic wiring of the health care system is now complete—a result of federal investment and lower technology prices. The need now is to harness the power of analytics to improve care.[236]

The most troubling aspect of the consolidation trend is evidence that mergers and acquisitions by hospitals and physician groups cause prices to rise and may even, in some cases, mean lesser quality. The group Catalyst for Payment Reform found that "by 2006, over 75 percent of US metropolitan [areas] had experienced enough hospital merger activity to be considered 'highly consolidated.' Nationwide, payments to hospitals on behalf of the privately insured are an estimated 3 percent higher than they would be absent hospital consolidation. In some specific cases, prices have gone up as much as 50 percent post consolidation." For example, "when two competing Northern California hospitals … merged, prices increased between 28 and 44 percent."[237]

Sherry A. Glied and Stuart H. Altman have observed that competition is essential to contain costs and improve quality and that it is "alarming that concentration is increasing throughout the hospital, physician, and insurer markets." While 75 percent of markets were highly concentrated in 2006, a decade later the percentage had climbed to 90. In addition, "65 percent of specialist physician markets, and 63 percent of insurance markets were highly concentrated in 2016. These rates are substantially higher than those observed just six years earlier."[238]

---

236 Samulson, "Is this the Future of Healthcare?"
237 Delbanco, et al., "Provider Consolidation and Health Spending: Responding to A Growing Problem."
238 Glied and Altman, "Beyond Antitrust: Healthcare and Health Insurance Market Trends and the Future of Competition."

We do not dispute these numbers, but we do argue that there are some inconvenient truths concealed within the data. In many cases health systems are punished by payers for being alone. When a standalone hospital joins a larger system, it is likely to receive higher payments from commercial insurers; payments that it did not have the marketplace clout to demand prior to consolidation. The general expectation in health care has been that mergers could generate savings due to consolidation of various services. But in many cases prices rise because the imbalance in power is rebalanced; the merger gives the smaller entity a new level of marketplace standing and, thus, greater reimbursements.

A second inconvenient truth involves the comparison of health care to other industries such as banking, for example, where mergers actually do increase productivity through the application of technology. In health care it's the opposite—the application of technologies increases costs, because medical technology—as opposed to information technology—is extremely expensive. And research scientists and device manufacturers are continually coming up with new and (often) better machinery which most organizations deem necessary notwithstanding the expense.

It is important to recognize as well that health care also suffers from "Baumol's disease," a malady defined by the late economist William Baumol, who taught at New York University and Princeton. Baumol explained "how technological advances raise productivity and naturally push up wages as workers are able to produce more goods ... But those same increases in productivity ... do not apply to labor-intensive activities like ... doctor examinations." What is the cure for the disease? There isn't one, Baumol said, and he "warned that the rising relative expense of health care, education, and other essential services ... would make them seem less and less affordable." Efforts to control the cost of health care, he argued, would be generally fruitless. "Cost increases are in the nature of the health care beast," he wrote in the *New York Times* in 1993. "Efforts to alter this nature will be fruitless or harmful." He wrote that "the real danger is that the nation, mistakenly thinking it must rein in runaway costs, will curtail valuable health services and render them inaccessible for the less affluent."[239]

The problem in the US today is not consolidation, per se, but consolidation *without integration* of health services.

The problem in the US today is not consolidation, per se, but consolidation *without integration* of health services. There is much evidence to date suggesting that consolidation by itself improves neither quality nor affordability. We argue, however, that consolidation when accompanied by integration can have a salutary effect on markets while at the same time insuring delivery of care to all communities, especially underserved areas. The promise of consolidation is the ability of integrated delivery systems to provide access to high quality, coordinated care. It is clear from our own experience at Northwell that integrated care improves health outcomes. With integration, large systems are able to provide all services including advanced specialization in heart disease, surgery, cancer care, etc. in departments specifically tailored for individual specialties. When an organization consolidates without integrating they may be able to leverage better payments and achieve some economies of scale. The much harder thing is to integrate throughout the organization so that you achieve the same standards of care everywhere.

Absent consolidation/integration, how will providers deliver the

239 Cohen, "William J. Baumol, 95, 'One of the Great Economists of His Generation,' Dies."

kinds of services consumers demand? The business of health care and the delivery of medical services has reached a point where it is too complex for a few doctors with a Mom-and-Pop operation. The need for new technologies alone can overwhelm a small practice financially. Standalone hospitals and individual physician practices are limited in doing what is required: delivering care to patients along a continuum where a primary care physician and team provide a central medical home to manage conditions and connect patients with the appropriate specialty care.

Many systems that claim to be integrated are far from it. Some of these are a system in letterhead only, places where acquisitions of smaller entities by a large medical center creates a feeder for the hub. As we look around, we see quite a number of health "systems" that, in reality, are freestanding silos independent of each other. How can consolidation succeed if smaller entities—community hospitals, for example—do not see the benefits to their patients? If they see only that their patients are used to build revenue for the mother ship? In a consolidated organization, success is possible only if every element within the organization—small- and medium-sized hospitals, specialty hospitals, physician practices, *everybody*—sees the benefits for patients, communities, and providers.

One of the greatest benefits of consolidation/integration comes from the kinds of advance research and innovation found in larger systems. Our colleague, Dr. Thomas McGinn, senior vice president and executive director of the Medicine Service Line at Northwell, puts it this way:

> If at the heart and soul of a lot of the consolidation is efficiency in patient experience, and, what I would call an update in the evidence that's occurring throughout that process, that's a great thing for everybody. If you're a private

physician, and this is not meant to be disparaging because my father was a private physician in the classic sense of the word and I thought he was a great doc. He kept up on his literature, so this is not across the board. But, in general, if you're sitting in a community and you're in practice for 20 or 30 years, you have a certain way of doing things and you get comfortable in those methods. But medicine changes.[240]

In a large system, especially one with a medical school, McGinn points out, there is an ongoing process to examine the latest research and innovations in care delivery:

Our job is to look at the recent evidence and the science and make sure that's being adopted across our sites. It's also a two-way street. There may be physicians in the community that say, 'look, this is the best way to do this. It's been studied, and we've adopted it. How come the system hasn't done it?' The complaint about consolidation is that you lose the personal touch of the local doctor and there was some of that—I get that. But, on the other hand, in a large integrated system you can raise the bar in terms of the quality and the adoption of the new evidence and science, and I think patients are better off for that.[241]

At Northwell, we are growing organically as well as through consolidation/integration. We make no apologies for this growth, which we believe is in the best interest of all our stakeholders—patients first and foremost, as well as the communities we serve. We don't want to get big for the sake of getting big. We build scale so

240 McGinn, interview with author.
241 Ibid.

we can innovate to improve outcomes across a broad swath of our geographic area. Scale is necessary to the extent that we integrate all of the pieces of our organization—so they work together to improve the health of our communities. Integration is about coordinating care, developing clinical protocols, and common, back-office functions that save money. It is no small thing that

> **Scale is necessary to the extent that we integrate all of the pieces of our organization—so they work together to improve the health of our communities.**

consolidation also saves some smaller hospitals that quite likely would have closed down absent a partnership with a larger entity. In a consolidated system, weaker partners can be nursed back to financial health over time, which is what we have seen in a number of cases within our own system. At Northwell, the concept of integration is central to what we do. So, what exactly do we mean when we use the term? How can you tell the difference between a consolidated organization and one that has integrated as well?[242]

One way to discern integration is to look under the hood and see what questions and issues were raised during the period when the consolidation was being considered. In a merger or acquisition purely designed to gain increased market share, the essential questions—in a way, the *only* questions—are financial. In a merger or acquisition where the more ambitious goal is *integration*, the questions are related to finances as well as mission and culture. Are the missions of the two organizations consistent? Would the acquisition/merger add value to *both* organizations? Is the organization being acquired one with a reputation for clinical quality? Is it a strong community partner? Is there a solid board and leadership team? An essential part

---

242 Dowling, "The Prizes and Pitfalls of Hospital Acquisitions."

of the due diligence involves looking closely at the culture of the new organization. Traditional due diligence is finance-centric. We do the numbers, of course, but we work just as hard on figuring out whether a new partner shares our personality and mission. There is no way to overstate the importance of culture in these matters. We suspect that many more mergers fail due to cultural issues than financial ones.

Based on our experience at Northwell—where we have grown to an integrated, twenty-three-hospital system—the transition process speaks volumes about whether there will be a merger or a successful integration. Some systems create transition teams responsible for the merger while the people who are actually running the business day-to-day are left out of the process. This is a bad omen. The people running the core day-to-day business of a hospital should be responsible for the integration, for they are the people who know the business best, and they are the ones who will have to live with the merger results.

There are, of course, drawbacks to consolidation. First and foremost, the work to integrate two organizations, particularly those with strongly held and differing cultures, is difficult. Finances present challenges as do issues of mission and culture. It is also often painful for a standalone entity to give up some of its identity. This is where hospital trustees are forced to make tough choices: *Do I vote to continue as an independent entity and risk potential reductions in services or even closure? Or do I vote to join a larger system and risk immersion into a corporate entity?*

A good example of what is possible with a large, integrated-delivery system involves the resurrection of Southside Hospital in Bay Shore, Long Island, New York. In the 1980s through the mid-90s, Southside was a financially distressed community hospital on the verge of bankruptcy. The organization was in such dire straits that at various points it was forced to sell hospital property to make payroll and to forego payment of Social Security taxes. Through this turmoil, Southside's reputation for clinical quality bottomed out.

At the point when Southside was about to go out of business, our organization stepped up and welcomed Southside into our network. Because of our size and financial strength, we were able to provide funding to stabilize Southside's finances and maintain the community's access to its varied services. Since 2007 we have invested more than $200 million in Southside, and in that time period occupancy has gone from 69 percent to 100 percent, and the number of employed physicians has gone from 42 to 208. Southside is now a level-II trauma facility with the ability to perform advanced cardiac surgery, including open-heart surgery. Without consolidation, it is likely that Southside Hospital—now the number-one hospital in Suffolk County, New York—would have ceased to exist by 2008 or earlier—a loss of varied health services for a large community along with a loss of an economic engine for the region.

Mergers are not the only way to partner with other provider organizations. We have a number of affiliations of different shapes and sizes, and a recent example suggests the benefits of such affiliations to all concerned. In early 2018 we entered into a collaboration agreement with the Western Connecticut Health Network, which includes three hospitals, six thousand, three hundred employees, and several dozen physician practices. The affiliation involves exploring joint clinical programs and collaboration to provide services to populations of patients especially under new, value-based-payment contracts. John Murphy, CEO of the Western Connecticut group, put the affiliation into perspective: "We are proactively managing our transition to value-based care by collaborating with local and regional organizations that share our vision and values. Leveraging Northwell's areas of expertise will enable us to sustain excellence and growth as the health care industry rapidly evolves."[243]

We make no pretension that our system here at Northwell is perfect, but we do believe that consolidation *with integration* has enabled us to connect the clinical dots—to link all the pieces along the clinical continuum of care to reduce variability and standardize care. Our size and integrated nature also enable us to expand services in underserved areas—something we would not be able to afford without the growth we have experienced. We have made significant investments in shifting from high-cost, inpatient settings to more affordable ambulatory care nearer to where patients live. In recent years, we have gone from 70 percent inpatient, 30 percent ambulatory, to nearly 50–50 as of 2018—thus moving care significantly closer to where our patients live. Scale has enabled us to both invest in research while building one of the leading health care educational systems in the United States. Scale has enabled our people to experiment—to try new things: to try and fail and try again. The harsh marketplace reality is that small, standalone entities struggling financially are able to do very few of these things. As a result, it is the residents of the communities served by the standalone entity who suffer.

In health care, it's not just provider organizations that are joining forces. The major pharmaceutical companies have consolidated to the point where there exist only a handful of major pharma entities, and the same is true in the national insurance marketplace. Even though federal judges rejected two proposed mega-mergers—between Cigna and Anthem and between Aetna and Humana—there remain only five major insurance players in the US. And with vertical mergers in process—between Cigna and Express Scripts and the acquisition

---

243 Western Connecticut Health Network, "WCHN and Northwell Health Establish Collaboration Agreement."

of Aetna by CVS—it is clear that on the pharma and insurance side of the industry there will only be a small handful of major players in the years to come. Some of the folks at Deloitte who study health care are bullish on this prospect:

> The siloes in the US health care system have been softening in recent years. That is a very positive trend. No single sector in isolation can materially address the cost, access, and quality challenges the industry faces. Perhaps most importantly, the convergence of the health-plan and provider sectors is likely to accelerate … This willingness to come together reflects the growing recognition that better synchronization between the financing and delivery of health care services and products is likely a necessary condition for systemic change. In many cases, convergence will be driven by various partnership approaches, including joint ventures, alliances, and a host of contractual arrangements.[244]

Whatever the arrangements, there is government oversight of health care that has become entirely too intrusive. Regulation is a necessary part of any industry, but in health care, over-regulation and misguided regulation stifles creativity and innovation. During a time when stakeholders are clamoring for changes to the health care system that deliver real value to consumers, it is up to providers to think outside the box and give people the care they deserve. Conversely, it's up to regulators to loosen their grip on the industry and let providers pursue innovative approaches that will enable them to get the best results.[245]

---

244 Scott, "2018 Health Plans Outlook."
245 Dowling, "The Issue of Ill-Conceived Regulation and How It Led to CareConnect's Demise."

CHAPTER NINE

Lifelong Learning: New Ways to Educate the Workforce

"If you want to change the way care is delivered you have to change the way caregivers are educated."

n medicine, where the pace of discovery moves at warp speed, how do you educate doctors, nurses, technicians, administrators—everybody? Not just in college or graduate school, but in an ongoing way for decades after graduation?

"Traditional systems for transmitting new knowledge—the ways clinicians are educated, deployed, rewarded, and updated—can no longer keep pace with scientific advances," according to a report from the Institute of Medicine. And for good reason. The "volume of the biomedical and clinical knowledge base has rapidly expanded, with research publications having risen from more than 200,000 a year in 1970 to more than 750,000 a year in 2010. The result is a paradox: advances in science and technology have improved the ability of the health care system to treat diseases, yet the sheer volume of new discoveries stresses the capabilities of the system to effectively generate and manage knowledge and apply it to regular care."[246]

It's not just advances in science that doctors, nurses, technicians, and administrators must keep up with. There are new technologies and new ways of practicing proactive, upstream medicine, new approaches and methods of paying for care, and new methods for measuring quality and the overall experience of care.

"Critics have long faulted US medical education for being hidebound, imperious and out of touch with modern health care needs," according to a report in the *Wall Street Journal*. "The core structure of medical school—two years of basic science followed by two years of clinical work—has been in place since 1910." Susan Skochelak, the American Medical Association's vice president for medical education, noted in the *Journal* article that there is concern that students are not learning enough about "the science of health care delivery. How do you manage chronic disease? How do you focus on prevention and wellness? How do you work in a team?"[247]

These concerns are very real, yet there is encouraging news: one of the more powerful trends in health care involves change in the ways caregivers are educated both in graduate school and over the course of a career.

"Developments both in technology and in our understanding of the human brain and learning processes are laying the groundwork for exponential change." It is clear that "a wave of innovation is sweeping through medical schools, much of it aimed at producing young doctors who are better prepared to meet the demands of the nation's changing health care system," according to the *Journal* article.[248]

---

246 Smith, et al., *Best Care at Lower Cost: The Path to Continuously Learning Healthcare for America*

247 Beck, "Innovation Is Sweeping Through US Medical Schools; Preparing Doctors—And in Greater Numbers—For New Technologies and Methods."

248 Ibid.

In the past couple of decades, there has been an explosion in the number of educational programs within health care organizations such as Cleveland Clinic, Mayo Clinic, Kaiser Permanente, Virginia Mason Medical Center, Geisinger Health System, Intermountain Health, and many others. New approaches to medical education include broader course work where, at Mayo Clinic, for example, students follow "a new course of study, called the Science of Healthcare Delivery, which will run through all four years and include health care economics, biomedical informatics and systems engineering." Schools are also breaking from the tradition of focusing on individual students to teaching teams. Dr. Wyatt Decker, chief executive of the Mayo Clinic in Arizona, told the *Journal* that "the old model was, you'd go on rounds; the attending would ask a question, and the young resident had to get the right answer. In the new model, you're part of a team, and somebody else might have the right answer."[249]

Medical schools are also "placing far less emphasis on memorizing facts, such as which drugs do what and how they interact with other drugs. Such information is now readily available electronically. 'The fund of medical knowledge is now growing and changing too fast for humans to keep up with, and the facts you memorize today might not be relevant five years from now,'" says NYU associate dean Dr. Marc Triola.[250]

Among the most dramatic shifts is a recognition by some medical schools that memorization is outmoded. In traditional medical education students spend countless hours memorizing facts and figures, only to forget many of them when it comes time to learn new material for their next exam and in an age when Google holds so many answers in a single click of the mouse, memorization is too often a waste of time.

---

249 Ibid.
250 Ibid.

Our colleague, Dr. Lawrence Smith, physician-in-chief at Northwell Health, brings interesting perspective:

> When I was in medical school, the best students in the class were defined by only one attribute, memory. If you could memorize millions of unrelated facts and spit them back on a test, you were considered the smartest kid in the room. I was studying one night and I was talking with my wife and I opened the phone book and she says, 'What are you doing?' I said, 'I am just going to memorize the whole phone book. I am getting really good at mindless memory.' In the age of the internet and smart phones you absolutely do not need memory. In fact, I would argue you should never *trust* memory except for the things you do all of the time. How do we teach the concepts of science that drive how the human body works? How do we teach science at the conceptual level and minimize the need to memorize minutiae, and at the same time give people robust enough concepts that if they wanted to do research in an area or look something up in an area, they can quickly teach themselves that minutiae because they understand the concepts.[251]

The task for students is not to memorize but to become adept at identifying the most reliable online sources of information ranging from Google to various scholarly journals available online.

Physicians of the future need to embrace a more interdisciplinary approach to delivering care than the purely clinical focus our medical schools have cultivated for decades. Thanks to the new wave of medical schools that offer joint medical degrees and other changes

---

251 Kenney, op. cit.

in the way we train doctors, new physicians are more diverse and well-rounded than we've seen in the past. Medical schools offering a mix of programs that include business, law, molecular medicine, and other advanced studies in conjunction with medical degrees will continue to become more appealing as physicians of the future seek more

Physicians of the future need to embrace a more interdisciplinary approach to delivering care than the purely clinical focus our medical schools have cultivated for decades.

options for professional growth. Of course, diversity not only relates to a physician's course of study but to the increasingly diverse patient populations served by providers.

With an increasingly diverse patient population, an essential aspect of learning involves understanding the social determinants of health (discussed in chapter 4).

"Part of preparing future physicians to deliver the best care is teaching them about the nation's vast variety of people, but understanding cultural differences requires more than just background in race, ethnicity and religion," according to an article on the AMA Wire. "Tomorrow's doctors are learning more about socioeconomic status, gender, sexual orientation and other social determinants of health. Physicians nationwide support integrating more training on the social determinants of health into undergraduate medical education."[252]

Dr. Karen Sheehan, professor of pediatrics and preventive medicine at Northwestern University's Feinberg School of Medicine, sees "a growing consensus that medical students should understand the social determinants of health in order to provide optimal care." She notes that most schools teach students about the social determinants

---

252 AMA Wire, "What Future Doctors Need to Know About Health Determinants."

but that many faculty members "are grappling with what to teach about this topic, how to teach it, and how to evaluate students' knowledge, skills, and attitudes ... There is not yet defined an optimal approach to teaching medical students about their role as physicians in addressing the social determinants of health. Most faculty were not formally taught about the social determinants of health in their training and learned of their role in addressing them through trial and error."[253]

Learning about the social determinants of health means recognizing a broader responsibility to the community outside of the school or hospital walls. Says Dr. Mark Schuster, founding dean of the Kaiser Permanente School of Medicine:

> Ultimately, we ... want to prepare students to be leaders in their communities. If they're in situations where local policies may influence the health of their patients, we want our graduates to work with lawmakers and local health department officials to address those problems. If we turn out outstanding physicians who go out and provide outstanding care to patients in communities across the country, while helping to make those communities more conducive to healthful living, then we will have done our job.[254]

Beyond reducing reliance on memorization and teaching the social determinants of health, there are numerous other fresh approaches to educating doctors that are at work throughout the country. A fundamental flaw in medical education has long been that students rarely had direct, meaningful interaction with patients until the third year of medical school. At the Zucker School of Medicine

---

253 Sheehan, *Optimizing Student Learning About the Social Determinants of Health*.

254 Rege, "Founding Dean Dr. Mark Schuster on what makes the Kaiser Permanente School of Medicine Stand Out."

at Hofstra/Northwell, however, students start their medical education with an accelerated Emergency Medical Technician training program followed by assignment to an ambulance crew. This puts students in contact with patients in real life situations—encounters that are often stressful and occasionally tragic. This face-to-face contact with patients during the earliest stages of medical school has proven deeply meaningful to students.

In medical school, "nobody remembers anything that is not related to patients," says Dr. Smith:

> I could say to 50 doctors, 'Tell me what you learned in the first two years of medical school,' and they would look at me and say, 'I don't remember a single day. I have no idea. I know I did really well on a test because I was a great crammer, but if I learned anything, I certainly do not remember it now.' Undoubtedly, you learn *something*, but they will tell you that 'I have *never forgotten* what I learned in the context of a real patient.' And not as an observer either. I mean directly involved with a patient. So if that is the case then why not embed real patients from day one?[255]

Dr. Smith offers an apt analogy: "Let's say you wanted to learn how to play baseball," he says, "and I said to you, 'Okay, I can teach you to play baseball. I want you to come to my baseball camp and every morning we will study the physics of fastballs, sliders, and curveballs.' You would learn some interesting things about different pitches but you would absolutely *not* learn how to hit a baseball."[256]

While students at the Zucker School of Medicine at Hofstra/Northwell learn on the front lines—as EMTs and also working side-

---

255 Kenney, op. cit.
256 Ibid.

by-side with physicians in one-on-one mentoring—they also learn in the classroom and, often, from one another. A case method (patient-centered explorations in active reasoning, learning, and synthesis) has students in small groups focus on a specific medical topic each week. Students begin the week going through two clinical cases, about four to five pages each, and conduct research on each case via whatever online sources they have found to be most informative, up-to-date, and reliable. With faculty guidance, students define learning objectives and report to classmates on particular elements of the case. Each student is responsible for learning all the material and reporting on a particular aspect of the case. The net result is that students are, in effect, teaching the material to one another, an indication that they have learned the material.

There are other notable innovations at the Zucker school and one, in particular, merits a mention. Dr. Smith, the medical school dean, and Dr. David Battinelli, associate dean, both believed that lectures in medical school were essentially a waste of time. Yet the notion that the curriculum would not include lectures—or would not include them as an essential teaching element—seemed nothing less than bizarre to most physicians. Lectures—with the "sage on the stage"—were the core of medical schools throughout the world. Smith and Battinelli found that in schools not requiring attendance at lectures, a majority of students stayed away. On average, only about one third of students at these institutions regularly attended lectures.

"At one of the very top medical schools less than 20 percent of the students are going to lectures yet they go on to become great doctors," says

> "At one of the very top medical school less than 20 percent of the students are going to lectures yet they go on to become great doctors."

Dr. Smith. "Maybe the students are telling you lectures are not the way they learn medicine." These students who avoided lectures were not lounging at the beach, says Battinelli, but finding information and insights on the internet.[257]

"With smart phones and computers people can look things up immediately and not have to go to lectures," he says. "If you want a lecture on cystic fibrosis from the expert at Stanford you can find it online in two seconds." Thus, at the Zucker School of Medicine at Hofstra/Northwell, there are no lectures.[258]

Since the founding of the Zucker School a number of other new medical schools have followed a similarly innovative path. Kaiser Permanente, the largest integrated health system in the United States, opened a new medical school in 2017 with "the idea of creating a school focused on teaching students about promoting health, not just treating disease," according to Dr. Schuster, founding dean. The emphasis is on "prevention, data analytics, population health and a commitment to underserved communities, among other health factors." The school also stresses "the importance of supporting the students, faculty, and staff in maintaining their own wellness."[259]

Dr. Schuster told an interviewer:

> When I went to medical school, we sat in class all day and there was one lecture after another, and many of us would just scribble down every word we could get, and then read over our notes later to start to process the information. But [at Kaiser Permanente Medical School] our plan is to take an approach of using small-group, case-based learning. We'll

---

257 Ibid.
258 Ibid.
259 Rege, op. cit.

also flip the classrooms, so students will have watched some videos, engaged in some exercises and done some readings in advance so they come to class having learned the basic facts, and then can process and consolidate what they've learned in interactive small groups. Students won't be sitting in the back of a large lecture hall falling asleep, passively absorbing but also often being disengaged. [At Kaiser Permanente], our goal is to provide students with the education strategies to become lifelong learners. Knowledge is changing too rapidly; we want to teach students how to access and assess information and continue to learn new techniques and procedures as the information becomes available.[260]

The idea of lifelong learning is one of the recurring themes in the latest thinking about educating caregivers. At Northwell, we have played a role in this movement with the creation and growth of the Center for Learning and Innovation. When we began the process of building a learning center nearly twenty years ago we paid close attention to the GE corporate education model. At GE, lifelong learning is at the core of the company's values. As far back as 1956 the company established a learning center at Crotonville, New York, a bucolic setting north of New York City. In the more than half century since its founding, Crotonville had become synonymous with excellence in corporate leadership education. GE executives recognized that personal growth and development of its leaders was essential to success.

The Crotonville educational approach aimed to help employees maximize their individual strengths and to set out on a journey that would elevate a career from a job to a meaningful life experience. That is what we wanted for the employees at Northwell—the kind of education

---

260 Ibid.

that would help them perform at the highest level to the benefit of the organization and to their own personal fulfillment. With guidance from the GE team at Crotonville as well as from faculty at the Harvard School of Public Health, we set out to establish an in-house learning center—the Center for Learning and Innovation.

Our Northwell team built the curriculum with the guidance of the GE consultants from Crotonville and faculty from the Harvard School for Public Health. "We relied on them to make sure that we were building something academically sound," says Kathleen Gallo, PhD, senior vice president and chief learning officer at Northwell. "We wanted to make sure we had the right principles." Gallo was guided, as well, by her own readings into the work of MIT faculty member Peter Senge, author of the landmark book *The Fifth Discipline: The Art and Practice of the Learning Organization*. Senge's thinking related to the power of meaning in work and the importance of learning within a professional setting.[261]

"When you ask people about what it is like being part of a great team, what is most striking is the meaningfulness of the experience," Senge writes in *The Fifth Discipline*. "People talk about being part of something larger than themselves."[262]

Gallo was drawn to Senge's definition of mastery and the need to pursue it within an educational setting: "People with a high level of personal mastery live in a continual learning mode," he wrote. "They never 'arrive'… personal mastery is not something you possess. It is a process. It is a lifelong discipline."[263]

The Center for Learning and Innovation is all about continuing the education process throughout a career for doctors, nurses,

261 Gallo, op. cit.
262 Senge, *The Fifth Discipline: The Art and Practice of the Learning Organization*.
263 Ibid.

technicians, and administrators. Courses range from patient safety to physician leadership, from bioskills to critical care. An essential aspect of the center involves the use of simulation, which Gallo learned about from Michael Barger, the chief learning officer at JetBlue University, the learning center training crew members. Barger was a former Navy pilot who told Gallo that simulation was an essential part of training elite Naval aviators. While simulation was a way of life in the Navy in particular, and aeronautics in general, it had yet to penetrate health care. The more Gallo examined the world of simulation the more convinced she grew that it could make a difference in quality and safety.

She says:

> We know that bringing a lot of people into a big room and lecturing to them for hours on end does nothing but demonstrate that the person in the front of the room is reinforcing his or her own knowledge. And while that person can leave and check the box that they taught that day, they cannot check the box and say with certainty that anybody *learned* that day. You need learner engagement right from the get go. If you were getting on a plane to go on vacation and the pilot said, 'Well, I just want to let everybody know you're in good hands. I attended every lecture that they gave and I earned a hundred on every test. I have never flown a plane but I did graduate number one in my class so I am sure everything will be fine. Please buckle up.'[264]

Activity-based learning is the process where clinicians or students, working on a simulated patient with a particular set of symptoms, experience the intensity and stress that concentrate the learner's mind. This is the kind of engagement from which people learn from the high-

---

264 Gallo, op. cit.

fidelity simulator, a plastic body connected to a computer capable of creating a variety of symptoms within the body. For example, the simulator-as-patient could talk and respond to questions. This was done via a staff member from the sim center in the control room. The simulated body was capable of having any heart rate, blood pressure, or pulse. In fact, almost any sort of challenging situation, including high-risk, rare events could be replicated in the simulation center. Gallo saw how simulated events could effectively create the "suspension of disbelief" essential to effective learning. While all the participants know very well that the "patient" in the bed is a plastic creation linked to computers, the literature notes that during the simulation process, a suspension of disbelief takes places among both students and experienced clinicians. This, in turn, creates an appropriate and realistic level of stress and enhances the learning process.

At the Center for Learning and Innovation all simulation sessions are recorded both with video and audio. Gallo learned from other industries, she says, that "the most important thing is after simulation, people sit down and go through a debriefing and the debriefing is much longer than the simulation, because that's where everybody learns." How were the most effective debriefings achieved? What were the approaches and techniques that worked best? What were the approaches to be avoided? The debriefs revealed the fault lines, the reflexive words or actions that doctors and other clinicians defaulted to in stressful situations.[265]

"The faculty members are not pointing out what an idiot you are, but actually formulating questions and facilitating the discussion, because you want the participants to self-discover," says Gallo. "During the debrief you ask questions such as, 'What went well for you? How did the whole thing feel?' And people pick up where

265 Ibid.

they could improve. No matter how experienced we are we always need practice," she says. "Research indicates that the way you create mastery is through deliberate practice. Look at professional athletes who practice much more than they play in games. The same with concert pianists, chess players, people at the top of their game. You have to deliberately practice what you want to master and you need continuous immediate feedback so you don't develop your own belief system that what you are doing is right."[266]

Medical and nursing schools along with provider organizations are rich with educational innovations. Added to traditional and non-traditional course offerings are Massive Open Online Courses (MOOC), where learners at various stages of a career can gain new knowledge and understanding chosen from an array of course offerings. The Institute for Healthcare Improvement also offers something akin to MOOC with the IHI Open School. Its course offerings have been taken by more than a half million health care professionals throughout the world. And it is no small matter that the Institute of Medicine has formally recognized the need for continuous learning throughout a career in health care. An IOM report includes a vision for "a learning health care system that links personal and population data to researchers and practitioners, dramatically enhancing the knowledge base on effectiveness of interventions and providing real-time guidance for superior care in treating and preventing illness. A health care system that gains from continuous learning is a system that can provide Americans with superior care at lower cost."[267]

---

266 Ibid.
267 Finkelman, *Quality Improvement: A Guide for Integration in Nursing.*

CHAPTER TEN

Unmistakable Progress: The Power of the Health Care Quality Movement

"The disrupters have improved health care in America—improved quality, safety, and access."

I n the short term, with the pace of modern life, it is easy to lose track of the arc of history—to miss the broader context of a story, particularly when it involves a health system comprising nearly one-fifth of the world's largest economy. It is especially easy to lose sight of the big picture amid the "persistent media attention to" the health system's "shortcomings and errors," as Paul Keckley put it. The decline narrative notwithstanding, historical perspective and context make clear that the US has come a very long way in improving health care. Anyone who lived through the 1960s and '70s has witnessed advances that are nothing short of astonishing.

Let's be more precise in our context and go back to the day when the course of medical history in the US shifted in a fundamental way. On November 30, 1999, front pages of newspapers across America reported the almost unfathomable news that America was in the midst of "an epidemic of medical errors." As we noted in chapter one, a report from the Institute of Medicine of the National Academies— "To Err Is Human: Building a Safer Health System"— found that not only was American medicine not as great as widely believed, but that doctors and hospitals were making errors—"stunningly high rates of medical errors"—so grievous that in the process of trying to heal they were killing as many as ninety-eight thousand people per year. The epidemic included "adverse drug events and improper transfusions, surgical injuries and wrong-site surgery … restraint-related injuries or death, falls, burns, pressure ulcers, and mistaken patient identities … in intensive care units, operating rooms, and emergency departments."[268]

The cost in human life and suffering represented by the statistics was painful for all involved, but there was more:

> Errors also are costly in terms of loss of trust in the health care system by patients and diminished satisfaction by both patients and health professionals. Patients who experience a long hospital stay or disability as a result of errors pay with physical and psychological discomfort. Health professionals pay with loss of morale and frustration at not being able to provide the best care possible. Society bears the cost of errors as well, in terms of lost worker productivity, reduced school attendance by children, and lower levels of population health status. A variety of factors have contributed to the … epidemic of medical errors," the report continued, including "the decentralized and fragmented nature of the health care delivery system—or 'nonsystem,' to some observers. When patients see multiple providers in different settings, none of

---

268 Institute of Medicine of the National Academies, "To Err Is Human: Building a Safer Health System."

whom has access to complete information, it becomes easier for things to go wrong.[269]

One of the central findings of the report indicated that the problem was caused by faulty systems rather than negligent individuals. "This is not a 'bad apple' problem," the report stated. "More commonly, errors are caused by faulty systems, processes, and conditions that lead people to make mistakes or fail to prevent them." In a damning indictment, the report found that "there is no cohesive effort to improve safety in health care."[270]

With the ink barely dry on "To Err Is Human," the Institute of Medicine followed with a second study in 2001, which concluded that not only was health care in the US unsafe, but the delivery system was basically a mess. "Crossing the Quality Chasm: A New Health System for the 21st Century," found:[271]

"The US health care-delivery system does not provide consistent, high-quality medical care to all people" and "too frequently and routinely fails to deliver its potential benefits. Indeed, between the health care that we now have and the health care that we could have lies not just a gap, but a chasm." The report

> **"Between the health care that we now have and the health care that we could have lies not just a gap, but a chasm."**

found that care in the US was insufficiently safe, effective, patient-centered, timely, efficient, and equitable and called for nothing less than "a fundamental, sweeping redesign of the entire health system."[272]

The combined messages of the two reports constituted a one-two

---

269 Ibid.

270 Ibid.

271 Institute of Medicine of the National Academies, "Crossing the Quality Chasm: A New Health System for the 21st Century."

272 Ibid.

punch to the gut of the health care universe. The message to patients was *beware*; to physicians and other care givers—*you are not getting the job done.* Reaction to the reports was mixed. Initially, particularly in the wake of "To Err Is Human," there was a sense of shock and confusion among many health care professionals. The notion that so many people were being harmed in places devoted to healing was, to say the least, disturbing. Some providers reacted with skepticism and denial, refusing to believe the analysis. But others—and it would prove to be tens of thousands of others throughout health care in the ensuing years—took the reports to heart and sought to fix the broken system.

A single example from that time embodies the spirit of the reform efforts across the country. This was one of countless improvement efforts where a doctor and his team focused on a very specific problem. Dr. Rick Shannon, who is currently (2018) at the University of Virginia, was a cardiologist at Allegheny General Hospital in Pittsburgh when one of his patients, awaiting a heart transplant, died due to an infection. Tragically, it turned out to be a preventable infection caused by the improper insertion of an IV. The idea that a patient so close to gaining a new heart would succumb as a result of something as seemingly simple as an improperly inserted IV shocked both the patient's family and medical team. And certainly, it stunned Dr. Shannon. It also sent him on a mission to try to understand and correct what had gone wrong. He spent months observing various medical teams inserting the types of major IVs known as central lines—and he found an alarming lack of consistency.

"What he saw was remarkable: Some doctors wore masks and caps, some didn't; some wore gowns, some didn't; some used special sterile drapes, some didn't; some used one form of disinfectant, others didn't. On top of all this, five different types of catheters were being used."[273]

---

273 Kenney, op. cit.

Shannon and his team "found fifty or sixty permutations of the way this was done. That creates such background chaos that *no one knows what the right way to do it is.*" No one at Allegheny had explored the best practices in medicine to determine what the safest way for inserting and caring for the lines would be. It was exactly the type of problem that was at the heart of the message in "To Err Is Human."[274]

After months of study, Shannon and his team reached a consensus on a standard approach: Doctors would wear masks, gowns, and caps, and the same disinfectant would be used each time. Patients would be draped, a particular catheter would be used, and so on. Over time, the team identified the best way to insert a central line, and the new goal was to follow that approach to the letter every time for every patient without exception. During the year prior to this work, there were forty-nine central-line infections in Shannon's unit. Two years later, there were two—followed by a period of more than two years without a single such infection. Multiply Rick Shannon's work by a thousand or ten thousand, and you begin to get a sense of the scope and intensity of the quality and safety movement in the wake of the double-whammy IOM reports.

Five years after the publication of "To Err Is Human," there was progress. The Commonwealth Fund reported that "notable advances have been made [including] the development of performance standards, an increase in error reporting, integration of information technology, and improved safety systems." Perfect? Far from it—very far from it. Nonetheless there was real, tangible progress.[275]

The Commonwealth Fund analysis found that "within months of the IOM report," Congress established a Center for Patient Safety

---

274 Ibid.
275 Bleich, "Medical Errors: Five Years After the IOM Report."

charged with 'a national effort to combat medical errors and improve patient safety.'" In the wake of the IOM reports came "unmistakable progress," wrote Dr. Robert Wachter, chair of the department of medicine at the University of California at San Francisco School of Medicine. Wachter saw "much stronger engagement" on safety issues from major organizations involved in the regulation, study, and governance of health care.[276]

Writing in *Health Affairs* in 2010, Wachter urged readers to:

> Think back to 1999. The Joint Commission inspected hospitals with preannounced surveys every few years. The Agency for Healthcare Research and Quality (AHRQ) supported virtually no research in patient safety. The World Health Organization lacked an organized safety enterprise. Physician and nurse accrediting boards and training programs did not include safety as a core competency. There was no federal effort to promote health IT implementation. Only cognoscenti had heard of the Institute for Healthcare Improvement, and the National Quality Forum had just been formed. Today, each of these organizations is flourishing, with much of their focus on patient safety … The IHI has completed two major campaigns that energized thousands of workers and health care organizations. AHRQ has supported myriad initiatives in safety—not just research but also Web sites, tools, and more. The National Quality Forum's list of 'never events' became the scaffolding for reporting systems and payment changes. The Joint Commission has modified its processes and recently formed a center to support safety and quality improvement. [There

---

276 Wachter, "Patient Safety at Ten: Unmistakable Progress, Troubling Gaps."

had been] unmistakable progress … If anyone had asked me in 1999 how much change in patient safety related areas would be possible within a decade, I would have greatly underestimated our actual accomplishments. Most of our changes have constituted real progress, and even our missteps have yielded valuable lessons.[277]

A decade-plus before Rick Shannon's work, and years before the IOM reports, a group of physicians from various parts of the United States gave birth to the health care-quality-reform movement. In the late 1980s and early 1990s, a relative handful of reformers gathered together to improve the quality and safety of care. The Pacific Business Group on Health was founded in 1989 to improve quality and affordability for large employers. The Institute for Healthcare Improvement, which began informally in the late 1980s, was officially formed in 1991. The leaders of IHI, notably Drs. Donald Berwick and Paul Batalden, played leading roles throughout the 1990s, and, in fact, Berwick was one of the lead authors of "To Err Is Human."

In the years after the two IOM reports were published, many different groups were formed, including a number we have mentioned in prior chapters: Catalyst for Payment Reform which focuses on accelerating toward paying for value rather than volume; the Health Transformation Task Force, formed in 2015 by major employers to improve quality and affordability; and the International Consortium for Health Outcomes Measurement, the Michael Porter-led group focused on identifying measures that matter most to patients. Disrupters at major medical groups including Johns Hopkins, Geisinger Health, HealthPartners in Minnesota, Intermountain Healthcare in

---

277 Ibid.

Utah, Kaiser Permanente in California, Virginia Mason Medical Center in Seattle, Cincinnati Children's Hospital Medical Center, and

The disrupters have improved health care in America— improved quality, safety, and access.

many others. The disrupters have improved health care in America— improved quality, safety, and access. The progress in recent decades is due, in large measure, to the men and women and their institutions who have militated against the status quo and done the research, experimentation, and measurement that makes progress possible. Disrupters promoting a reform agenda have:

- advocated for greater attention to behavioral health in primary care;

- identified the social determinants of health as essential elements within a patient profile;

- changed the way care is measured from doctor-centered to patient-centered;

- identified new ways of educating the health care workforce;

- consolidated and in some cases integrated large provider groups;

- changed the way we pay for (some) care;

- and in the process of working on all of these issues, the quality movement has grown to become an important force in American health care.

At Northwell Health, we count ourselves among the disrupters pursuing the reform agenda. We have a unique obligation in our region as the largest provider of health care in New York State (Northwell is comprised of twenty-three hospitals, 640 ambulatory sites, and forty-three urgent-care centers) as well as the state's largest private employer—sixty-six thousand men and women working at our hospitals, outpatient facilities, research centers, and medical and nursing schools. We are working on advancing all of the trends with more success on some than others. We think of ourselves as quite advanced in terms of the consolidation/integration trend, and we have had success both with technology (including telehealth) and integrating behavioral health into primary care. We aspire to do better on social determinants and increasing the amount of our work that involves payment reform. We are acutely aware each day of our need to do better on all fronts.

In order to plot the pathway forward, let's focus on another specific date: on January 30, 2018, Amazon, Berkshire Hathaway, and JP Morgan Chase & Co. announced a venture to partner "on ways to address health care for their US employees, with the aim of improving employee satisfaction and reducing costs. The three companies ... will pursue this objective through an independent company that is free from profit-making incentives and constraints. The initial focus of the new company will be on technology solutions that will provide US employees and their families with simplified, high-quality and transparent health care at a reasonable cost."[278]

Is there any company in America that embodies the concept of disruption more than Amazon? It is because of Amazon's innovative nature along with the leadership of Jeff Bezos, Warren Buffet, and Jamie Dimon that the announcement of their collaboration received such widespread attention, though reaction was not entirely positive.

"People are inclined to credit Amazon with magic, but who knows if it will extend to this line of work?" said Mark Pauly, a

---

278 Business Wire, "Amazon, Berkshire Hathaway, and JPMorgan Chase & Co. to Partner on US Employee Healthcare."

professor at the Wharton School at the University of Pennsylvania. "The public announcement only talks about assembling smart people and giving them resources—which has been tried already by insurers, delivery systems, and the government through Medicare—and it has not worked. So, this is a bet on pixie dust."[279]

Another observer suggested they might be doing little more than "tinkering at the edges" of health care. But, these companies don't generally do pixie dust, nor do they tinker around the edges—unless you consider disrupting the entire American retail sector a form of tinkering.[280]

Success in this venture, said Bezos, will require "a long-term orientation." Along with patience, these companies bring a laser-like customer focus to the task, something to which health care organizations around the country aspire. And it is no small thing that Amazon also brings its one hundred million-strong Amazon Prime customers. If health care in the future is about data, technology, and trusting relationships, then Amazon brings real value.

The companies also, as the *Times* noted, "bring successful management, technological expertise, and substantial capital to the venture." The marketplace power of this coalition was in part measured by the stock market reaction to the announcement that the three were teaming up." Big stock market moves after the announcement suggest that investors think that whatever the companies develop could become broadly adopted."[281]

The group, in Buffet's words, "does not come to this problem with answers" but rather with a belief "that putting our collective

---

279 Knowledge@Wharton, "Will Amazon, Berkshire Hathaway, and JPMorgan Reinvent Healthcare?"

280 Ibid.

281 Sanger-Katz and Abelson, "Can Amazon and Friends Handle Healthcare? There's Reason for Doubt."

resources behind the country's best talent can, in time, check the rise in health costs while concurrently enhancing patient satisfaction and outcomes." Bezos spoke of the need for "a long-term orientation." However, it was Dimon who made the most revealing statement of all: that "our goal is to create solutions that benefit our US employees, their families and, potentially, *all Americans* [emphasis added]."[282]

Interestingly, many news reports made it appear as though the three are doing something brand new, but the reality is that they are newcomers to an already robust and growing reform movement. As we have seen in previous chapters, the three companies are following in the footsteps of others that have already succeeded in disrupting aspects of the status quo. It cannot be denied, however, that these companies and their leaders bring something special to the cause. Certainly, they bring a fair amount of bargaining power on behalf of their 1.1 million employees, and that adds marketplace muscle to the movement. But their value goes beyond their numerical strength. What new thinking might they bring to the cause? What would be the equivalent disruption in health care to what Amazon has done in retail? Ultimately, what alchemy comes from collaboration among the three companies and their leaders? And how will this lead to further collaboration with other major players in the quality movement?

To what extent the new entity will engage with other players is uncertain, but surely, they will take to heart the many lessons that have been learned over the years of the movement from the likes of Boeing, Walmart, Intel, The Pacific Business Group on Health, the Institute for Healthcare Improvement, the National Quality Forum, and other disrupters who have thought long and hard about how to accelerate the megatrends.

"We are interested in exploring ways we can work together,

---

282 Ibid.

and I trust that we will," says Rob Andrews, CEO of the Health Transformation Alliance, a membership organization which includes companies such as American Express, Caterpillar, and JP Morgan.[283]

One obvious potential innovation would be for Amazon to establish a pharmacy business employing its distribution network to deliver medications. David Lareau, CEO of the health care company Medicomp, offered some thoughts in early 2018 on the matter:

> Given their well-established nationwide delivery infrastructure and e-commerce network, Amazon has the potential to quickly disrupt the distribution of medications ... as well as medical supplies, durable medical equipment, and other commodity goods. Berkshire Hathaway ... brings deep expertise in risk management, which could prove valuable when creating and managing delivery models that encompass outcomes-based reimbursement and risk sharing. ... J.P. Morgan Chase offers deep financial resources that could support a variety of initiatives, including self-insurance underwriting.[284]

Another strength of the coalition is its leader. Dr. Atul Gawande is a surgeon at Brigham & Women's Hospital in Boston, and is widely known throughout the health care universe as the author of superb articles in *The New Yorker* and books on various aspects of health care. Dr. Gawande is an interesting choice to lead the venture. He has never run a large organization, certainly never been the CEO of a health system or insurance company—and that may be, in part, why he was chosen by Bezos, Buffett, and Dimon. Gawande is a professor at Harvard Medical School, from which he graduated, as well as a

---

283 Ibid.
284 Lareau, "Is It Any Surprise that Corporate Giants Are Taking on Healthcare?"

MacArthur "genius grant" recipient and a Rhodes Scholar. He is, by any measure, a brilliant polymath who has been thinking, writing, and speaking thoughtfully about the challenges in the US system for many years. Soon after he was hired, he told an interviewer that his job in the new venture is "to figure out ways that we're going to drive better outcomes, better satisfaction with care, and better cost efficiency with new models that can be incubated *for all* [emphasis added]."[285]

From where we sit, it seems clear that the trends about which we write in this book are helping to lead our system in the direction Gawande describes—toward better outcomes, satisfaction, and cost efficiency. What, exactly, Gawande will do remains unclear, but our general sense of optimism about the major trends in health care spills over into a sense of hope about the Amazon venture and the ability of Atul Gawande to lead it in interesting and productive directions.

We have focused to a significant extent on the movement that includes private entities such as corporate employers, health systems (mostly not-for-profit), think tanks, and other activists aligned in pursuit of the reform agenda. But it should also be noted that the federal government plays an important role in the movement as well. The Centers for Medicare & Medicaid Services has fostered multiple innovations that help advance the megatrends. CMS and the Center for Medicare and Medicaid Innovation deserve credit for the good work that has been done particularly in pursuit of shifting from volume-based payments to value-based payments. More broadly, the federal government, through the Affordable Care Act, enabled millions of Americans to get much-needed insurance coverage.

Government also plays a critically important role as regulator of

---

285 Tracer, "Amazon-Berkshire-JPMorgan Health Venture Takes Aim at Middlemen."

the industry, and in this role the government could do much better. Greater flexibility in rules and regulations would save providers from a mountain of paperwork and the restrictions that constrain appropriate risk-taking and innovation.

The federal government has been among the pioneers in advocating for a shift from paying for volume to paying for value, and if the Amazon coalition is going to have a broad impact in the world of health care they would be well-advised to push hard in this direction. How so, exactly? During a Harvard Business School forum David Lansky, chairman of the Pacific Business Group on Health, outlined five essential elements that, from a purchaser's standpoint, should be in place:[286]

1. Significant dollars must be at risk.

2. Focus on improvement cannot come from within.
   "In all the examples I know of where purchasers have driven payment reform, they have crossed their fingers hoping providers would figure out what to do—and it hasn't worked," Lansky explains. The purchasers must specify what they want providers to work on.

3. Purchasers must work together.
   "They have to lock arms and send a consistent and comprehensive signal to a market," says Lansky, so that providers stop inadvertently blocking transformation by cutting a discount in one area and making it up elsewhere.

4. They must measure outcomes. Being accountable and paid for, outcomes will trigger new thinking about how to organize care.

---

286 Lansky, op. cit.

5. They must compete with one another. Administered price-setting and negotiated prices by plans exist, but transparent competition on price does not.

While we like much of what David Lansky has to say, we have a fundamental disagreement with his second point. His implication that purchasers are the only innovators is contradicted by countless innovations from provider groups throughout the country. We know, in our own case, for example, that significant innovation at Northwell has come from within and had no connection to any sort of stipulations by purchasers.

One of the most damning indictments with "To Err Is Human" was the finding in 1999 that "there is no cohesive effort to improve safety in health care." Look at how far we have come. As of late 2018 not only is there a cohesive effort to improve safety, but there is also a sprawling movement across the country seeking to improve quality, affordability, access, equity—every aspect of American health care. And the movement is gaining strength. The Amazon trio moves the health care reform movement closer to a place it has always aspired to be—in the mainstream of American business; not something that was an HR initiative, but, rather, something that brought the focus, energy, and attention of the C-suite to the health care arena. We noted earlier that the trends are not self-sustaining. Major players, including employers and the government, must press forward to advance the trends. Perhaps Bezos, Buffet, and Dimon can bring a new level of energy to the effort.[287]

Whatever happens with Amazon, Berkshire, and Morgan, the broader movement soldiers on. And the implications of that movement

---

287 Institute of Medicine of the National Academies, op. cit.

are tangible and present at the frontlines of care, where millions of Americans receive superb care for heart disease, cancer, and many other maladies; where behavioral health services are more available in primary care settings than ever before; where providers take into account the social determinants of health and where advanced technologies are linking patients to their care teams; where education of the health care workforce is more robust than ever, and where measures that matter most to patients are in the spotlight; where consolidation of health care organizations make the integration of services more likely; and where we move closer each day to a system where we pay for value rather than volume more than ever before.

ACKNOWLEDGMENTS

We are grateful to many of our colleagues here at Northwell Health including Jeff Kraut, Dr. Lawrence Smith, Howard Gold, Terry Lynam, Don Simon, and Dr. Kris Smith, all of whom read portions of the manuscript and offered thoughtful comments. We are grateful for insights from many colleagues including Drs. David Battinelli, Joseph Conigliaro, Martin Doerfler, Joanne Gottridge, Mark Jarrett, Barry Kanzer, Thomas McGinn, Jonathan Merson, Ira Nash, Ram Raju, Manish Sapra, Kevin Tracey, and John Young, as well as to Kathleen Gallo, Sven Gierlinger, James Kostolni, Ramon Soto, and Katherine Zimmerman. We received thoughtful feedback and guidance from Bill Kramer at the Pacific Business Group on Health. We are grateful to Dr. Arnold Baskies of the American Cancer Society, Dr. Vincent Bufalino at the American Heart Association, Sean Duffy at Omada Health, Dr. Rick Lopez at Atrius Health, Dr. Steven Nissen at Cleveland Clinic, and Dr. Rishi Manchanda at HealthBegins. Thanks go to Mara Laderman, Dan Schummers, and Jane Roessner at the Institute for Healthcare Improvement; Virna Little at the Institute for Family Health in New York; Anne Fields and Diane Powers at the University of Washington; Suzanne Delbanco at Catalyst for Payment Reform; Ben Isgur at

PWC's Health Research Institute; Dr. Dan Lessler at the Washington State Healthcare Authority; Rick Pollack at the American Hospital Association; Brenda Reiss-Brennan at Intermountain Health; Chas Roades, CEO at Gist Healthcare; and Jeff Micklos and Clare Wrobel at the Healthcare Transformation Task Force.

BIBLIOGRAPHY

AIMS Center. "Impact: Improving Mood – Promoting Access to Collaborative Treatment." University of Washington. https://aims.uw.edu/impact-improving-mood-promoting-access-collaborative-treatment.

AMA Wire. "What Future Doctors Need to Know About Health Determinants." November 20, 2014. https://wire.ama-assn.org/education/what-future-doctors-need-know-about-health-determinants.

Aston, Geri. "Closing the Behavioral Health Gap Through Collaboration." Hospitals and Health Networks. May 24, 2017. https://www.hhnmag.com/articles/8211-closing-the-behavioral health care-gap-through-collaboration.

Battinelli, David. Interview with author. 2018.

Baskies, Arnold. Interview with author. 2018.

Beck, Melinda. "Innovation Is Sweeping Through US Medical Schools; Preparing Doctors—And in Greater Numbers—For New Technologies and Methods." *Wall Street Journal.* February 16, 2015. https://www.wsj.com/articles/innovation-is-sweeping-through-u-s-medical-schools-1424145650.

Beck, Melinda. "What Measures Should Be Used to Evaluate Healthcare?" *Wall Street Journal.* March 22, 2015. https://www.wsj.com/articles/what-quality-measures-should-be-used-to-evaluate-healthcare-providers-1427079654.

Bermingham, Neesan, Katrine Bosley, and Samarth Kulkarni. "Realizing the Potential of CRISPR," interview by McKinsey. McKinsey and Company. January 2017. https://www.mckinsey.com/industries/pharmaceuticals-and-medical-products/our-insights/realizing-the-potential-of-crispr.

Bleich, Sara. "Medical Errors: Five Years After the IOM Report." Commonwealth Fund. July 2005. https://www.commonwealthfund.org/publications/issue-briefs/2005/jul/medical-errors-five-years-after-iom-report.

Boynton, Ann, and James C. Robinson. "Appropriate Use of Reference Pricing Can Increase Value." *Health Affairs*. July 7, 2015. https://www.healthaffairs.org/do/10.1377/hblog20150707.049155/full.

Brown, David. "As Healthcare Quality Rises, So Does Price." *Washington Post*. July 26, 2009. http://www.washingtonpost.com/wp-dyn/content/article/2009/07/25/AR2009072502381.html?hpid=topnews.

Brown, Patricia Leigh. "Cod and 'Immune Broth': California Tests Food as Medicine." *New York Times*. May 11, 2018. https://www.nytimes.com/2018/05/11/health/food-as-medicine-california.html.

Business Wire. "Amazon, Berkshire Hathaway, and JPMorgan Chase & Co. to Partner on US Employee Healthcare." January 30, 2018. https://www.businesswire.com/news/home/20180130005676/en/Amazon-Berkshire-Hathaway-JPMorgan-Chase-partner-U.S.

Casalino, Lawrence P., David Gans, Rachel Weber, Meagan Cea, Amber Tuchovsky, Tara F. Bishop, Yesenia Miranda, Brittany A. Frankel, Kristina B. Ziehler, Meghan M. Wong1, and Todd B. Evenson. "US Physician Practices Spend More Than $15.4 Billion Annually to Report Quality Measures." *Health Affairs* 35, no. 3. March 2016. https://doi.org/10.1377/hlthaff.2015.1258\.

Castelucci, Maria. "Will CMS' Efforts to Limit Quality Reporting to 'Meaningful Measures' pay off? Stakeholders Aren't Sure." *Modern Healthcare*. January 24, 2018. http://www.modernhealthcare.com/article/20180120/NEWS/180129995.

Centers for Disease Control and Prevention. "HAI Data and Statistics." https://www.cdc.gov/hai/surveillance/index.html.

Centers for Medicare and Medicaid Services. "New Participants Join Several CMS Alternative Payment Models." January 18, 2017. https://www.cms.gov/Newsroom/MediaReleaseDatabase/Press-releases/2017-Press-releases-items/2017-01-18.html.

Cohen, Patricia. "William J. Baumol, 95, 'One of the Great Economists of His Generation,' Dies." *New York Times*. May 10, 2017. https://www.nytimes.com/2017/05/10/business/economy/william-baumol-dead-economist-coined-cost-disease.html.

Cold Spring Harbor Laboratory. "125 Years: Discoveries that Made a Difference 1890-Now." Accessed 2018. http://labdish.cshl.edu/discoveries/timeline/.

Compton-Phillips, Amy. "The 'Give a Darn' Method for Outcomes Measurement," interviewed by Tom Lee. *NEJM Catalyst*. February 8, 2018. https://catalyst.nejm.org/give-darn-method-outcomes-measurement/.

Coutré, Lydia. "Cleveland Clinic CEO Sees 'Total Restructuring' Ahead for HealthCare Business." Modern Healthcare. October 24, 2017. http://www.modernhealthcare.com/article/20171024/NEWS/171029946.

Cuckler, Gigi, Andrea M. Sisko, John A. Poisal, Sean P. Keehan, Sheila D. Smith, Andrew J. Madison, Christian J. Wolfe, and James C. Hardesty. "National Health Expenditure Projections, 2017–26: Despite Uncertainty, Fundamentals Primarily Drive Spending Growth." *Health Affairs* 37, no.3. February 2018. https://doi.org/10.1377/hlthaff.2017.1655.

Cunningham, Peter J., Tiffany Green, and Robert T. Braun. "Income Disparities in the Prevalence, Severity, and Costs of Co-Occurring Chronic and Behavioral Health Conditions." *Medical Care Journal* 52, no. 2. February 2018: 139–145. https://doi.org/ 10.1097/MLR.0000000000000864.

Cutler, David. "Are the Benefits of Medicine Worth What We Pay for It?" Syracuse University Center for Policy Research. 2004.

Cutler, David. "The Highest Quality at a Lower Cost? We Don't Have That Yet." Interview with Patrick Conway. *NEJM Catalyst*. November 20, 2017. https://catalyst.nejm.org/patrick-conway-qa-cms-highest-quality-lowest-cost/.

Dafny, Leemore. *Payment Reform is a Play We're All Watching*. (Boston, Massachusetts: Navigating Payment Reform for Providers, Payers, and Pharma. November 2, 2017). 11:14.

Delbanco, Suzanne F., Robert Galvin, and Robert Murray. "Provider Consolidation and Health Spending: Responding to A Growing Problem." Health Affairs. November 14, 2012. https://www.healthaffairs.org/do/10.1377/hblog20121114.025308/full/.

DeVita Jr., Vincent T., and Elizabeth DeVita-Raeburn. *The Death of Cancer*. (Crichton Books, November 2015).

Doerfler, Martin. Interview with author. 2018.

Dowling, Michael J. "The Issue of Ill-Conceived Regulation and How It Led to CareConnect's Demise." *Becker's Hospital Review*. September 25, 2017. https://www.beckershospitalreview.com/hospital-management-administration/michael-dowling-the-issue-of-ill-conceived-regulation-and-how-it-led-to-careconnect-s-demise.html.

Dowling, Michael J. "The Prizes and Pitfalls of Hospital Acquisitions." *Becker's Hospital Review*. January 17, 2018. https://www.beckershospitalreview.com/hospital-management-administration/michael-dowling-the-prizes-and-pitfalls-of-hospital-acquisitions.html.

Duffy, Sean, and Thomas Lee. "In-Person Healthcare as Option B." *The New England Journal of Medicine* 378, no. 2. January 11, 2018: 104–106.

Emmanuel, Ezekiel. *Prescription for the Future.* (Public Affairs, 2017): 33.

Easterbrook, Gregg. *It's Better Than it looks: Reasons for Optimism in an Age of Fear.* (New York City: Public Affairs, 2018).

Farmer, Paul. "Investigating the Root Causes of the Global Health Crisis: Paul Farmer on the TED Book *The Upstream Doctors*." TED Blog. June 5, 2013. https://blog.ted.com/investigating-the-root-causes-of-the-global-health-crisis-paul-farmer-on-the-upstream-doctors/.

Finkelman, Anita. *Quality Improvement: A Guide for Integration in Nursing.* (Jones & Bartlett Learning, 2018): 32-33.

Frakt, Austin, and Ashish K. Jha. "Face the Facts: We Need to Change the Way We Do Pay for Performance." *Annals of Internal Medicine* 168, no. 4. November 2017: 291–292. https://doi.org/10.7326/M17-3005.

Frakt, Austin. "How Common Procedures Became 20 Percent Cheaper for Many Californians." *New York Times*. August 8, 2016. https://www.nytimes.com/2016/08/09/upshot/how-common-procedures-got-20-percent-cheaper-for-many-californians.html.

Frakt, Austin. "Medical Mystery: Something Happened to US Health Spending After 1980." *New York Times*. May 14, 2018. https://www.nytimes.com/2018/05/14/upshot/medical-mystery-health-spending-1980.html.

Frye, W. Bruce. *Caring for the Heart: Mayo Clinic and the Rise of Specialization.* (Oxford University Press, 2015).

Fryhofer Sandra L., Meena Seshamani, Karen B. DeSalvo, and Patrick H. Conway. "Progress and Path Forward on Delivery System Reform." *NEJM Catalyst*. October 18, 2017. https://catalyst.nejm.org/delivery-system-reform-progress-path/.

Glied, Sherry A., and Stuart H. Altman. "Beyond Antitrust: Healthcare and Health Insurance Market Trends and the Future of Competition." *Health Affairs* 36, no. 9. September 2017. https://doi.org/10.1377/hlthaff.2017.0555.

Gold, Rachel. Interview with author. 2018.

Gold, Rachel. "Addressing Social Needs to Improve Health at Kaiser Permanente and Beyond." Kaiser Permanente Center for Health Research. December 13, 2017. https://research.kpchr.org/News/CHR-Stories/Post/2501/Addressing-Social-Needs-to-Improve-Health-at-Kaiser-Permanente-and-Beyond.

Greater New York Hospital Association. "Statement on Gun Violence as Adopted by the Greater New York Hospital Association Executive Committee on March 1, 2018." http://www.gnyha.org/wp-content/uploads/2018/03/GNYHA-Statement-on-Gun-Violence-3-1-18.pdf.

Greene, Jan. "When Value Is in the Eye of the Patient." *Managed Care*. March 4, 2018. https://www.managedcaremag.com/archives/2018/3/when-value-eye-patient.

Haefner, Morgan. "Seventy-One Percent of Physicians Practice Revenue Tied to Fee-for-Service in 2016." Beckers Hospital Review. January 3, 2018. https://www.beckershospitalreview.com/finance/71-of-physician-practice-revenue-tied-to-fee-for-service-in-2016-ama.html.

Haefner, Morgan. "Survey: Most Americans with High-Deductible Health Plans Don't Shop for Care: 5 Things to Know." Becker's Hospital CFO Report. November 29, 2017. https://www.beckershospitalreview.com/finance/most-americans-with-high-deductible-health-plans-don-t-shop-for-care-5-things-to-know.html.

Harrison, Marc. "It's Past Time to Include Mental Health Into the Doctor's Office Visit." STAT News. August 25, 2017. https://www.statnews.com/2017/08/25/mental health-doctor-visit/.

Hartocollis, Anemona. "Cold Spring Harbor Lab, Seeking Human Subjects, Teams Up with Hospital System." *New York Times*. April 2, 2015. https://www.nytimes.com/2015/04/03/nyregion/cold-spring-harbor-lab-seeking-human-subjects-teams-up-with-hospital-system.html.

Harvard Business School Institute for Strategy and Competitiveness. "International Consortium for Health Outcomes Measurement." Accessed 2018. https://www.isc.hbs.edu/about-michael-porter/affiliated-organizations-institutions/Pages/ichom.aspx.

Health Leads. "Kaiser's Center for Total Health Highlights Health Leads as Innovative Healthcare Solution." February 12, 2014. https://healthleadsusa.org/2014/02/kaiser-permanentes-center-for-total-health-highlights-health-leads-as-innovative-healthcare-solution/.

HealthBegins. "Overview." accessed 2018. https://www.healthbegins.org/.

Henry J. Kaiser Family Foundation. "Health Insurance Coverage of the Total Population," trend graph. Accessed 2018. https://www.kff.org/other/state-indicator/total-population/?currentTimeframe=0&sortModel=%7B%22colI d%22:%22Location%22,%22sort%22:%22asc%22%7D.

Hsu, John, Mary Price, Christine Vogeli, Richard Brand, Michael E. Chernew, Sreekanth K. Chaguturu, Eric Weil, and Timothy G. Ferris. "Bending the Spending Curve by Altering Care Delivery Patterns: The Role of Care Management Within A Pioneer ACO." *Health Affairs* 36, no. 5. May 2017. https://doi.org/10.1377/hlthaff.2016.0922.

ICHOM. "Why Measure Outcomes?" Accessed 2018. http://www.ichom.org/why-measure-outcomes/.

Improving Chronic Illness Care. "The Chronic Care Model." Accessed 2018. http://www.improvingchroniccare.org/index.php?p=the_chronic_caremodel&s=2.

Institute of Medicine of the National Academies. "Crossing the Quality Chasm: A New Health System for the 21st Century." March 2001. http://www.nationalacademies.org/hmd/~/media/Files/Report%20Files/2001/Crossing-the-Quality-Chasm/Quality%20Chasm%202001%20%20report%20brief.pdf.

Institute of Medicine of the National Academies. "To Err Is Human: Building a Safer Health System." 2000. http://www.nationalacademies.org/hmd/~/media/Files/Report%20Files/1999/To-Err-is-Human/To%20Err%20is%20Human%201999%20%20report%20brief.pdf.

Jarrett, Mark. Interview with author. 2018.

Jenny Cordina, Rohit Kumar, and Christa Moss. "Debunking Common Myths About Healthcare Consumerism." McKinsey and Co. December 2015. https://www.mckinsey.com/industries/healthcare-systems-and-services/our-insights/debunking-common-myths-about-healthcare-consumerism.

Kamal, Rabah. "Medicare Thirty-Day Hospital Readmission Rates Have Declined." Peterson-Kaiser Health System Tracker. April 21, 2017. https://www.healthsystemtracker.org/chart/medicare-30-day-hospital-readmission-rates-declined/.

Kantarjian, Hagop. "An Unhealthy System." *US News and World Report.* May 30, 2014. https://www.usnews.com/opinion/articles/2014/05/30/no-the-us-doesnt-have-the-best-healthcare-system-in-the-world.

Karagianis, Liz. *The Brilliance of Basic Research.* (Spectrum, 2014).

Keckley, Paul. "Radical Incrementalism or System Redesign: Which Way Foreward for US Healthcare." The Keckley Report. April 23, 2018. http://www.paulkeckley.com/the-keckley-report/2018/4/23/radical-incrementalism-or-system-re-design-which-way-forward-for-us-healthcare.

Keckley, Paul. "Myth No. 1: Quality of Care in the US Health System is the Best in the World." The Healthcare Blog, March 6, 2018, http://www.paulkeckley.com/the-keckley-report/2018/3/5/xilzrf2j54ano1q8vdzlt55u6l7l50.

Kenney, Charles. *Disrupting the Status Quo: Northwell Health's Mission to Reshape the Future of Health Care.* (Productivity Press: May 15, 2017).

Kirschenbaum, Ira H. "Landmarks in Orthopedics: A Twenty-Year Perspective." *Medscape.* April 24, 2015. https://www.medscape.com/viewarticle/843690.

Klein, Sarah, and Martha Hostetter. "In Focus: Integrating Behavioral Health and Primary Care." Commonwealth Fund. August 28, 2014. https://www.commonwealthfund.org/publications/newsletter/2014/aug/focus-integrating-behavioral health-and-primary care.

Klein, Sarah, and Martha Hostetter. "Integrating Behavioral Health and Primary Care." Commonwealth Fund. September 2014. https://www.commonwealthfund.org/publications/newsletter/2014/aug/focus-integrating-behavioral health-and-primary care.

Knowledge@Wharton. "Will Amazon, Berkshire Hathaway, and JPMorgan Reinvent Healthcare?" February 6, 2018. http://knowledge.wharton.upenn. edu/article/will-amazon-berkshire-hathaway-and-jpmorgan-change-the-game-for-healthcare/.

Kochanek, Kenneth D., Sherry L. Murphy, Jiaquan Xu, and Elizabeth Arias. "Mortality in the United States, 2016." Centers for Disease Control and Prevention, NCHS Data Brief 293. December 2017. https://www.cdc.gov/nchs/ products/databriefs/db293.htm; Centers for Disease Control and Prevention found that average life expectancy at birth fell in 2016 by 0.1 years, to 78.6, after a similar drop in 2015. In twenty-five other developed countries, life expectancy in 2015 was 81.8 years.

Kolata, Gina. "A Medical Mystery of the Best Kind: Major Diseases Are in Decline." *New York Times*. July 8, 2016. https://www.nytimes.com/2016/07/10/ upshot/a-medical-mystery-of-the-best-kind-major-diseases-are-in-decline. html.

Kowalczyk, Liz. "Report Faults Children's Hospital for Medication Errors." Boston Globe. May 27, 2018. https://www.bostonglobe.com/metro/2018/05/27/ report-faults-children-hospital-for-medication-errors/HypBfWEJEGW5CJd-vlnCIDI/story.html.

Kramer, Bill. Interview with author. 2018.

Laderman, Mara. Interview with author. 2018.

Laderman, Mara, and Kedar Mate. "Integrating Behavioral Health into Primary Care." *Healthcare Executive* 2, no. 29. 2014: 74-77. http://www.ihi.org/ resources/Pages/Publications/IntegratingBehavioralHealthPrimaryCare.aspx.

Landro, Laura. "How Apps Can Help Manage Chronic Diseases." *Wall Street Journal*. June 25, 2017. https://www.wsj.com/articles/ how-apps-can-help-manage-chronic-diseases-1498443120.

Lansky, David. *Solving the Payment Problem: A Purchaser's Perspective*. (Boston, Massachusetts: Navigating Payment Reform for Providers, Payers, and Pharma. November 2, 2017). 8:18.

Lareau, David. "Is It Any Surprise that Corporate Giants Are Taking on Healthcare?" MedCity News. March 29, 2018. https://medcitynews.com/2018/03/ surprise-corporate-giants-taking-healthcare.

Leemore Dafny, and Namita Seth Mohta. "New Marketplace Survey: What's Next for Payment Reform?" *NEJM Catalyst.* November 20, 2017. https://catalyst.nejm.org/new-marketplace-survey-next-payment-reform/.

Liptak, Kevin. "Trump: 'Nobody knew health care could be so complicated.'" CNN. February 28, 2017. https://www.cnn.com/2017/02/27/politics/trump-health care-complicated/index.html.

Lopez, Rick. Interview with author. 2018.

Manchanda, Rishi, and Guy Roz. "How Can Your Home Make You Sick?" October 21, 2016. In TED Radio Hour. Podcast. MP3 audio. 9:15. https://www.npr.org/templates/transcript/transcript.php?storyId=497847442.

Mankiw, N. Gregory. "Beyond those Healthcare Numbers." *New York Times.* November 4, 2007. https://www.nytimes.com/2007/11/04/business/04view.html.

Markets Insider. "US Healthcare System Ties 29 Percent of Payments to Alternative Payment Models," press release. October 30, 2017. http://markets.businessinsider.com/news/stocks/u-s-healthcare-system-ties-29-of-payments-to-alternative-payment-models-1006178330.

McGinn, Thomas. Interview with author. 2018.

Mukherjee, Siddhartha. *The Emperor of All Maladies.* (New York: Simon & Schuster, 2011): 301.

National Cancer Institute. "Targeted Cancer Therapies." Accessed 2018. https://www.cancer.gov/about-cancer/treatment/types/targeted-therapies/targeted-therapies-fact-sheet.

National Health Policy. "Dispelling the Myths and Stigma of Mental Illness: The Surgeon General's Report on Mental Health." *National Health Policy* Forum 754. April 14, 2000: 1–7. http://www.nhpf.org/library/issue-briefs/IB754_SGRptMental_4-14-00.pdf.

NEJM Catalyst event "Expanding the Bounds of Care Delivery: Integrating Mental, Social, and Physical Health," held at Vanderbilt University Medical Center, January 25, 2018.

Nissen, Steven. Interview with author. 2018.

Nodell, Bobbi. "Wayne Katon Obituary." University of Washington Medical School. March 3, 2015. https://newsroom.uw.edu/story/wayne-katon-who-expanded-care-mental health-dies.

Noether, Monica, and Sean May. "Hospital Merger Benefits: Views from Hospital Leaders and Econometric Analysis." Charles River Associates. January 2017. https://www.crai.com/sites/default/files/publications/Hospital-Merger-Full-Report-_FINAL-1.pdf.

Noseworthy, John. *Telemedicine Will Increase Access to Care, Reduce Costs.* (Twin Cities Pioneer Press: June 5, 2016).

Omada Health. "Scientific Games." omadahealth.com. Accessed 2018. https://go.omadahealth.com/scientificgames.

Payne, Elizabeth. "A Brief History of Advances in Neonatal Care." NICU Awareness. January 5, 2016. https://www.nicuawareness.org/blog/a-brief-history-of-advances-in-neonatal-care.

Pear, Robert. "Medicare Allows More Benefits for Chronically Ill, Aiming to Improve Care for Millions." *New York Times.* June 24, 2018. https://www.nytimes.com/2018/06/24/us/politics/medicare-chronic-illness-benefits.html.

Pinker, Steven. *Enlightenment Now.* (London: Penguin Publishing Group, 2018).

Pinkner, Steven. *Enlightenment Now: The Case for Reason, Science, Humanism, and Progress.* (Viking: February 13, 2018).

Powers, Diane. Interview with author. 2018.

Press, Matthew J., Ryan Howe, Michael Schoenbaum, Sean Cavanaugh, Ann Marshall, Lindsey Baldwin, and Patrick H. Conway. "Medicare Payment for Behavioral Health Integration." *New England Journal of Medicine* 376. February 2, 2017: 405–407. https://doi.org/ 10.1056/NEJMp1614134.

Raju, Ram. Interview with author. 2018.

Rege, Alyssa. "Founding Dean Dr. Mark Schuster on what makes the Kaiser Permanente School of Medicine Stand Out." Becker's Hospital Review.

Reinhardt, Uwe. "Health Reform in America." *American Health Drug Benefits 1,* no. 3. April 2008.

Robert Wood Johnson Foundation. "Health Care's Blind Side." December 1, 2011. https://www.rwjf.org/en/library/research/2011/12/health-care-s-blind-side.html.

Rosenthal, Elisabeth. *An American Sickness: How Healthcare Became Big Business and How You Can Take It Back.* (New York: Penguin Press, 2017).

Samulson, Robert. "Is this the Future of Healthcare?" *Washington Post.* November 1, 2017. https://www.washingtonpost.com/opinions/is-this-the-future-of-health care/2017/11/01/45dcc4dc-bf1b-11e7-8444-a0d4f04b89eb_story.html?noredirect=on&utm_term=.5faad5f14d4e.

Sanger-Katz, Margot, and Reed Abelson. "Can Amazon and Friends Handle Healthcare? There's Reason for Doubt." *New York Times.* January 30, 2018. https://www.nytimes.com/2018/01/30/upshot/can-amazon-and-friends-handle-healthcare-theres-reason-for-doubt.html.

Sapra, Manish. Interview with author. 2018.

Schwenk, Thomas. "Integrated Behavior and Primary Care." *JAMA* 316, no. 8. August 2016: 822–823. https://doi.org/10.1001/jama.2016.11031.

Scott, Greg. "2018 Health Plans Outlook." Deloitte. January 9, 2018. https://deloitte.wsj.com/cio/2018/01/09/2018-health-plans-outlook/.

Senge, Peter. *The Fifth Discipline: The Art and Practice of the Learning Organization.* (Currency: 1990).

Shah, Nirav R., Artair J. Rogers, and Michael H. Kanter. "Healthcare that Targets Unmet Social Needs." *NEJM Catalyst.* April 13, 2016. https://catalyst.nejm.org/healthcare-that-targets-unmet-social-needs/.

Shaywitz, David A. "Doctor Android." *Wall Street Journal.* January 12, 2015. https://www.wsj.com/articles/book-review-the-patient-will-see-you-now-by-eric-topol-1421106779.

Shaywitz, David. "A Nuanced Take on Healthcare Consumerism." *Forbes.* December 14, 2015. https://www.forbes.com/sites/davidshaywitz/2015/12/14/a-centrist-perspective-on-healthcare-consumerism/#2da3f2a65a82.

Shaywitz, David. "A Nuanced Take on Healthcare Consumerism." *Forbes*. December 14, 2015. https://www.forbes.com/sites/davidshaywitz/2015/12/14/a-centrist-perspective-on-healthcare-consumerism/.

Shaywitz, David. "At J.P. Morgan, A Sense that the Long-Promised Biotech Future Has Arrived; Is Tech Disruption Next?" *Forbes*. January 13, 2018. https://www.forbes.com/sites/davidshaywitz/2018/01/13/at-j-p-morgan-a-sense-that-the-long-promised-biotech-future-has-arrived-is-tech-disruption-next/#6ee7503a2c0f.

Sheehan, Karen. *Optimizing Student Learning About the Social Determinants of Health*. video, 1:16. http://www.feinberg.northwestern.edu/sites/cpci/hrsa-grant/student-learning-about-the-social-determinants-of-health.html.

Sheth, Kevin. "Too Many People Die from Strokes Because Treatment Is Delaye." *Washington Post*. April 6, 2018. https://www.washingtonpost.com/national/health-science/too-many-people-die-from-strokes-because-treatment-is-delayed/2018/04/06/d5ea0c5e-329a-11e8-94fa-32d48460b955_story.html?utm_term=.bc3ddb69f445.

Sidney, Stephen, Charles P. Quesenberry Jr., Marc G. Jaffe, Michael Sorel, Mai N. Nguyen-Huynh, Lawrence H. Kushi, Alan S. Go, Jamal S. Rana. "Recent Trends in Cardiovascular Mortality in the United States and Public Health Goals." *JAMA Cardiology* 1, no. 5. June 29, 2016, doi:10.1001/jamacardio.2016.1326.

Singer, Natasha. "How Big Tech Is Going After Your Healthcare." *New York Times*. December 26, 2017. https://www.nytimes.com/2017/12/26/technology/big-tech-healthcare.html.

Skillrud, Ion, Wendy Gerhardt, and Maulesh Shukla. "The Great Consolidation: The Potential for Rapid Consolidation of Health Systems." Deloitte. 2014. https://www2.deloitte.com/content/dam/Deloitte/us/Documents/life-sciences-healthcare/us-lshc-great-consolidation-111214.pdf.

Slotkin, Jonathan R., Olivia A. Ross, M. Ruth Coleman, Jaewon Ryu. "Why GE, Boeing, Lowe's, and Walmart Are Directly Buying Healthcare for Employees." *Harvard Business Review*. June 08, 2017. https://hbr.org/2017/06/why-ge-boeing-lowes-and-walmart-are-directly-buying-healthcare-for-employees.

Smith, Kris. Interview with author. 2018.

Smith, Mark, Robert Saunders, Leigh Stuckhardt, and J. Michael McGinnis. *Best Care at Lower Cost: The Path to Continuously Learning Healthcare for America.* (National Academies Press, 2013).

Span, Paula. "Going to the Emergency Room Without Leaving the Living Room." *New York Times.* November 4, 2016. https://www.nytimes.com/2016/11/08/health/older-patients-community-paramedics.html.

Specter, Michael. "The Gene Hackers." *New Yorker.* November 16, 2015. https://www.newyorker.com/magazine/2015/11/16/the-gene-hackers.

Susan Dentzer, "Reform Chronic Illness Care? Yes, We Can," *Health Affairs* 28, no. 1 (January/February 2009): https://doi.org/10.1377/hlthaff.28.1.12.

Sven Gierlinger. Interview with author. 2018.

The Commonwealth Fund. "US Health System Ranks Last Among Eleven Countries on Measures of Access, Equity, Quality, Efficiency, and Healthy Lives." June 16, 2014. https://www.commonwealthfund.org/press-release/2014/us-health system-ranks-last-among-eleven-countries-measures-access-equity.

The Lancet. "Artificial Intelligence in Health Care: Within Touching Distance." *The Lancet* 10114, no. 390. December 23, 2017. doiI: 10.1016/S0140-6736(17)31540-4.

Thompson, Derek. "Healthcare Just Became the US's Largest Employer." *Atlantic Monthly.* January 9, 2018. https://www.theatlantic.com/business/archive/2018/01/healthcare-america-jobs/550079/.

Topol, Eric. "The Smart-Medicine Solution to the Healthcare Crisis." *Wall Street Journal.* July 7, 2017. https://www.wsj.com/articles/the-smart-medicine-solution-to-the-healthcare-crisis-1499443449.

Tracer, Zachary. "Amazon-Berkshire-JPMorgan Health Venture Takes Aim at Middlemen." Bloomberg News. June 24, 2018. https://www.bloomberg.com/authors/AP-470EpPkQ/zachary-tracer.

Tracey, Kevin. Interview with author. 2018.

University of Utah Health. "Algorithms for Innovation." Accessed 2018. http://uofuhealth.utah.edu/innovation.

US Bureau of Labor Statistics. "Fastest Growing Occupations." Accessed 2018. https://www.bls.gov/emp/tables/fastest-growing-occupations.htm.

Wachter, Robert M. "Patient Safety at Ten: Unmistakable Progress, Troubling Gaps." *Health Affairs* 29, no. 1. January 2010. https://doi.org/10.1377/hlthaff.2009.0785.

Wall Street Journal. "Doctors Debate Electronic Health Records," letter to the editor. April 9, 2018. https://www.wsj.com/articles/doctors-debate-electronic-health-records-1523277236.

Western Connecticut Health Network. "WCHN and Northwell Health Establish Collaboration Agreement," press release. February 8, 2018. https://www.westernconnecticuthealthnetwork.org/newsroom/article-listing/wchn-and-northwell-health-establish-collaboration-agreement.

INDEX